LETTERS TO SOLOVINE

Für die Fleischere
New Jock!

Dem alten Freund Solovine
A. Einstein 1946

Meinem lieben Solovine
A. Einstein 46.

Albert Einstein

LETTERS TO SOLOVINE

With an Introduction
by
Maurice Solovine

Philosophical Library
New York

Translated by Wade Baskin from the French
Lettres à Maurice Solovine.

Library of Congress Cataloging-in-Publication Data

Einstein, Albert, 1879-1955.
  Letters to Solovine.

  Translation of: Lettres à Maurice Solovine.
  1. Einstein, Albert, 1879-1955—Correspondence.
  2. Solovine, Maurice—Correspondence.
  3. Physicists—Correspondence. I. Solovine,
  Maurice. II. Title.
  QC16.E5A4   1986   530'.092'4   86-30573
  ISBN 0-8022-2526-8

Introduction

When I went to Berne as a student at the beginning of the century, I had not decided on the subjects that I wished to study. Since philosophy, though unworthy of the distinction today, still held claim to the study of the most exalted problems, I felt strongly inclined toward this subject, but simultaneously I had a burning desire to learn about concrete things, with the result that along with courses in Greek philosophy, literature and philology, I also studied mathematics, physics, and geology as well as a course in physiology in the Faculty of Medicine. By dint of hard work, I managed to acquire during the first year a body of knowledge which was far from enough to bring complete satisfaction but which allowed me to untangle the jumbled ideas that filled my head and to become aware of the paths and procedures through which the mind achieves positive results. My course in experimental physics had been absorbing, but the professor seemed to delight in speaking disdainfully of physical theories. He used to say that physical theories are more or less arbitrary constructions based on hypotheses and that the discovery of new facts undermines them and causes them to collapse, while facts which are carefully studied experimentally and shaped analytically stand as a definitive acquisition of physics and contribute to its continuous elaboration.

But what I found most absorbing were these theories, for they gave me an overall view of nature and a firm basis for the study of philosophy, but I felt incapable of understanding them because of a deficiency in mathematics; still, I tried hard to grasp as much as I could. The discovery of radium caused considerable agitation since it was thought to reverse the principle of the conservation of energy.

Having bought a newspaper and started to walk down the streets of Berne one day during the Easter vacation of 1902, I came to a place which said that Albert Einstein, a former student of Zurich Polytechnical School, would teach physics for three francs an hour. I mused: "Perhaps this man could explain theoretical physics to me." I made my way to the house mentioned in the advertisement, walked up to the second floor and rang the bell. I heard a thunderous *"Herein!"* and soon saw Einstein appear. The hallway was dark and I was struck by the extraordinary radiance of his large eyes. After I had gone inside his apartment and taken a seat, I told him that I was studying philosophy but wanted also to delve into physics so as to acquire a thorough understanding of nature. He confessed that he, too, had leaned toward philosophy when he was younger, but that the vagueness and arbitrariness that characterizes philosophy had turned him away from it and that he now concentrated exclusively on physics. For two hours we talked on about all sorts of questions and felt that we shared the same ideas and a mutual attraction. As I started to take leave of him, he went along with me and we continued the discussion in the street for about half an hour and agreed to meet the following day.

When we saw each other again, we renewed our discussion of certain questions that we had broached the preceding evening and the physics lesson was completely forgotten.

And when I came to him on the third day, he told me, after we had talked for a while: "As a matter of fact, you don't have to be tutored in physics; our discussion of problems that stem from it is much more interesting. Just come to see me and I will be glad to talk with you." I went back many times, and the better I became acquainted with him, the stronger my attachment grew. I admired his singular insight and his surprising mastery of physical problems. He was not a brilliant orator and did not use striking imagery. He outlined his subjects in a slow, even tone but in a remarkably lucid manner. To make his abstract thought more easily understood he sometimes used examples drawn from common experiences. Einstein was a skilled mathematician but he often spoke out against the abuses of mathematics in the hands of physicists. "Physics," he would say, "is basically a concrete, intuitive science. Mathematics is only a means to express the laws that govern phenomena."

As we were talking one day, I asked him: "Don't you think that it would be a good idea for both of us to read one of some great thinker's works, and then discuss the problems dealt with in the work?" "That's an excellent idea," he answered. I suggested then that we read a scientific work by Karl Pearson and Einstein eagerly accepted. A few weeks later, Conrad Habicht, whom Einstein had known in Schaffhouse and who had come to Berne to finish his studies with a view to teaching mathematics in the lycée, took part in our discussions. Our dinners were models of frugality. The menu ordinarily consisted of one bologna sausage, a piece of Gruyére cheese, a fruit, a small container of honey and one or two cups of tea. But our joy was boundless. The words of Epicurus applied to us: "What a beautiful thing joyous poverty is!"

Einstein was a candidate for a license at the time I knew him and was impatiently awaiting appointment. He had to give private lessons in order to live, and pupils were not easy to find; rates were low. One day when we were discussing ways of earning a living, he told me that the easiest way would be to play the violin in the streets. My answer was that if he had really decided to do that, I would begin to learn the guitar and accompany him.

Our material status was certainly unenviable, but we shared an uncommon penchant for studying and explaining the most difficult problems of science and philosophy. Together we read, after Pearson, Mach's *Analysis of Sensations* and *Mechanics* which Einstein had browsed through previously, Mills' *Logic*, Hume's *Treatise on Human Nature*, Spinoza's *Ethics*, some of Helmholtz' memoirs and lectures, some chapters from

André-Marie Ampère's *Essay on Philosophy*, Reimann's *On the Hypotheses Which Serve as a Basis for Geometry*, some chapters from Avenarius' *Critique of Pure Experience*, Clifford's *On the Nature of Things in Themselves*, Dedekind's *What Are Numbers?*, Poincaré's *Science and Hypothesis*, which engrossed us and held us spellbound for weeks, and many other works. We also read literary works such as Sophocles' *Antigone*, Racine's *Andromaque*, Dickens' *Christmas Tales*, most of *Don Quixote*, etc. Our meetings were sometimes highlighted by Einstein's playing some musical selection on his violin.

Unfortunately, it is impossible for me to set down the long, animated discussions provoked by the works which we read together. We would read a page or half a page—sometimes only a sentence—and the discussion would continue for several days when the problem was important. I often met Einstein at noon as he left his desk and renewed the discussion of the previous evening: "You said..., but don't you think...?" Or: "I'd like to add to what I said yesterday...."

The end of the nineteenth century and the beginning of the twentieth witnessed the flowering of research on the bases and principles of the sciences. We devoted weeks to the discussion of David Hume's eminently penetrating criticism of conceptions of substance and causality. Book III of Mills' *Logic*, which deals with induction, also held our interest for a long time.

Einstein favored the genetic method in the examination of basic ideas. To explain those ideas, he would call upon what he had observed among children. He also talked about his own works from time to time, and this revealed a brilliant mind and great originality. In 1903 he published his remarkable work entitled *Theories der Grundlagen der Thermodynamik*; in 1904, his *Allge-*

meine molekulare Theorie der Wärme; and in 1905, his admirable monograph entitled *Elektrodynamik bewegter Körper*, in which he outlined his theory of relativity. It is worth noting that no one except Max Planck has grasped the extraordinary significance of this work.

The extent to which Einstein could become absorbed in an interesting problem is suggested by our experience with caviar. In our strolls through the arcades of Berne we passed by a delicatessen where we saw, among other rare foods, some caviar on display. On seeing it, I remembered how much I had enjoyed it at home as a youth. It had been moderately priced there in Rumania, but in Berne it was too expensive for me to buy. This did not prevent me from extolling the merits of caviar in Einstein's presence. "Is it so good as all that?" he asked. "You just can't imagine how delicious it is," I answered. One day in February, I said to Habicht: "Let's plan a big surprise for Einstein. Let's serve him some caviar on his birthday, which comes on March 14." Whenever Einstein ate an unusual dish, he would become effusive and describe it in glowing terms. We were pleased by the thought of seeing him wax ecstatic and use the most far-fetched words to express his satisfaction. When March 14 came, we went to his apartment to dine together. I pretended that I was putting bologna sausages and the regular fare on the table; actually, I put the caviar in our three dishes, and then went over to speak with Einstein. That evening, he happened to start talking about Galileo's principle of inertia, and whenever he dealt with a problem, Einstein forgot completely about the earth and its joys and sorrows. When we sat down at the table, Einstein consumed bite after bite of caviar without saying anything about it, continuing his discussion of the principle of inertia. Habicht and I looked furtively at each other in amazement, and when Einstein had eaten all the caviar, I exclaimed: "Say, do you know what you have been eating?" "For goodness sake," he said, "it was that famous caviar." And after a minute of stunned silence, he added: "It doesn't matter. There's no point in serving the most exquisite delicacies to hicks; they can't appreciate them."

But we were still determined to have him enjoy caviar. A few days later we brought him a sizable portion of caviar, and to avoid having him treat it with shocking indifference, we intoned to the theme of the third movement of Beethoven's *Symphony in F*: "Now we are eating caviar...now we are eating caviar...." While eating, Einstein remarked: "I admit that it's a fine dish, but you have to be an accomplished epicure like Solovine to make so much fuss over it."

What stamped our Academy, as we jokingly referred to our meetings every evening, was the burning desire to broaden and deepen our knowledge and our affection for each other. I followed these meetings with intense interest, and amazingly enough, Einstein was as intensely interested in them as I and would not allow me to be absent. The one time that I missed a meeting cost me dearly.

Berne was outstanding in that leading violinists, cellists and pianists who were touring Europe from East to West, North to South, or vice versa, always gave one or two recitals there. We always made it a point to attend some of the recitals. One day I saw from the billboard that the widely-acclaimed Czech Quartet was going to give a recital. The program was very interesting; they were to perform quartets by Beethoven, Smetana and Dvořák. On arriving at Einstein's place for our regular meeting that evening, I told him the good news and told him that I intended to reserve three seats. "It seems to me," he said, "that it's better to give up that idea and read Hume, who is extremely interesting." "Good," I assured him. "It's a date." But I passed by the recital hall on the day mentioned in the announcement and was so affected by the sight of the program that I went into the vestibule mechanically and asked the lady in charge of ticket sales if any seats for the evening were still available.

Glancing at the seating chart, she called out the available seats in the different categories. When she finally added that she still had two specials, that is, seats for those without much money, I lost my head and bought a ticket.

As our "academic" meeting was supposed to be held at my place that evening, I rushed home to prepare dinner. Knowing that they were fond of hard-boiled eggs, I added four to the meal and placed them on a dish which I covered with a white sheet of paper on which I had written: *Amicis carissimis ova dura et salutem* (hard eggs and a greeting to very dear friends).

I then advised the lady in charge of the lodging house to tell them that I begged them to excuse my absence, an urgent matter having obliged me to leave. When she told this story, they understood. They conscientiously ate everything on the table. Then, knowing how I detested tobacco in any form, they began to smoke like persons possessed, Einstein his pipe and Habicht his thick cigars. They put the butts and smoldering pipe dumpings into a saucer and dumped the table, chairs, dishes, forks, cups, teapot, sugar bowl and a number of books on the bed; finally, they pinned to the wall a sheet of paper on which they had written: *Amico carissimo fumum spissum et salutem* (thick smoke and a greeting to a very dear friend).

After attending a musical event, I usually stroll around for a little while mulling over what I have heard and memorizing the themes, variations, etc. That was what I did after the recital given by the Czech Quartet. I walked slowly through the streets until around one o'clock in the morning. When I returned home and opened the door to my room. I thought that I would suffocate because of the heavy tobacco smoke. I threw the window wide open and began to remove from the bed the heap that reached almost to the ceiling. When I finally went to bed, the pillows and draperies reeked so strongly of the horrid tobacco fumes that I could not close my eyes. It was almost dawn before I managed to go to sleep.

When I went to Einstein's place for dinner and our "academic" meeting the next evening, he took one look at me, frowned, and shouted: "Wretch! You dare miss a regular meeting and listen to violin playing? Barbarian! Boor! If you ever again indulge in such folly, you will be excluded and shamefully expelled from the Academy."

Since the previous meeting had not been held because of my absence, this evening's session lasted until one o'clock in the morning.

After Einstein received his license, he married Mileva Maric, a young Serbian girl whom he had met at the Polytechnical School where she was studying. This event occasioned no change in our meetings. Mileva, intelligent and reserved, listened attentively but never intervened in our discussions.

After our "academic" meetings during the summer, we sometimes went up on Gurten, a sprawling mountain located south of Berne, to see the sunrise. The sight of the twinkling stars made a strong impression on us and led to discussions of astronomical questions. We would reach the summit at dawn and marvel at the sun as it came slowly toward the horizon and finally appeared in all its splendor to bathe the Alps in a mystic rose. We would wait for the restaurant located there to open, drink dark coffee and start our downward trek, arriving at the foot of the mountain around nine o'clock, dead tired but very happy.

We also went on hikes to Thun, a town located some thirty kilometers from Berne. We would leave at six o'clock in the morning and reach Thun around noon. Our view of the Alps occasioned discussions of their formation and structure and of geological problems in general. After breakfast, we would stay on the banks of Lake Thun until evening and return to Berne by train.

Such was the full and interesting intellectual life that we led for more than three years. Smitten by the desire to assimilate the culture of France, which has always exerted a strong attraction on Rumanians, I left Einstein in November, 1906, to study at the University of Lyons. I was saddened by the thought of being far from him and denied the pleasure of being present at our incomparable meetings, which ended with my departure and that of Habicht, who had left Berne several months before me. I have always been astounded by the fact that Einstein, crowned with renown and honors, still harbored nostalgic memories of our meetings.

I loved him and admired him profoundly for his basic goodness, his intellectual genius and his indomitable moral courage. In contrast to the lamentable vacillation that characterizes most so-called intellectuals, he fought tirelessly against injustice and evil. He will live in the memory of future generations not only as a scientific genius of exceptional stature but also as an

epitome of moral greatness. His portrait is deeply etched in my mind and, strangely moved, I whisper these words of Epicurus:
Sweet is the memory of a departed friend.

M. Solovine

LETTERS TO SOLOVINE

Lieber Solovine!

Ich denke oft an Sie und frage mich hin und her, was Sie wohl treiben mögen, und wie Sie Ihre Tage verbringen. Nun kommt noch ein kleiner äusserer Anlass hinzu zu dieser meiner Neugier und deshalb schreibe ich Ihnen.

Vor einigen Tagen präsentirte mir nämlich ein hiesiger Patentanwalt, den ich einerzeit auf Sie aufmerksam gemacht hatte, ein Schriftstück, welches in ein tadelloses Französisch übersetzt werden sollte. Natürlich passte mir das Ding nicht an, da die Angelegenheit pressierte. Aber ich will Sie nun doch fragen, ob Sie eine einigermassen zufriedenstellende Existenz gefunden haben. Wenn nein, so haben Sie hier nach

Berne, Friday
May 3, 1906

Dear Solovine,

I often think of you and wonder from time to time what you are doing and how you spend your days. I am writing you because of this and something else which has come up.

A few days ago a patent attorney to whom I had previously mentioned your name came to me with a document which was to be translated into flawless French. Naturally, I did not accept, for the matter was urgent. But I want to ask you if you are leading a satisfactory existence now. If not, here you still have a definite opportunity to find employment in the patent office and eventually work up to a good position. Write soon and let me know what you think of it.

All three of us are fine. The filius has already become a haughty, impertinent young chap. At the moment, I myself am not achieving many results from the scientific point of view, and soon I shall reach the stagnant and sterile age at which the revolutionary mentality of youth is deplored. My works are highly esteemed and are giving rise to further research. Professor Planck (Berlin) has written to me recently concerning this.

wie vor eine gewisse Chance, in
einem Patentbureau Beschäftigung,
mit der Zeit auch eine sichere Anstellung
zu finden. Schreiben Sie mir bald, was
Sie davon meinen.

Uns[3] geht es immer gut. Der filius
ist schon ein recht stattlicher, imper-
tinenter Kerl geworden. Mir selbst
gerät gegenwärtig nicht gerade viel in
wissenschaftlicher Beziehung, bald komm
ich schon ins stationäre und sterile
Alter, wo man über reaktutionäre
Gesinnung der Jungen wehklagt...
Meine Arbeiten finden viel Würdigung
und geben Anlass zu weiteren Unter-
suchungen. Prof. Planck (Berlin) schrieb mir
neulich darüber.

Ich bin schon wieder umgezogen,
diesmal wieder ins Kirchenfeld (Aegertenstr. 53). Seit Sie fort sind, ver-

kehre ich privatim mit keinem
Menschen mehr. Nun haben sogar
die Hedwey - Gespräche mit Besso
aufgehört. von Habicht habe ich
absolut nichts mehr gehört.

Von Ihrem guten Examen habe
ich durch H. Besso mit grossem Ver
gnügen vernommen. Hoffentlich wird
es Ihnen eine behaglichere materielle
Existenz eintragen

Seien Sie herzlich gegrüsst und
schreiben Sie bald
Ihrem A. Einstein.
Meine Frau sowie Herr Besso lassen
freundlich grüssen.

I have again moved, this time back to Kirchenfeld (Aegertenstr. 53). Since you have been gone, in my private life I have had nothing at all to do with anyone. Even my conversations with Besso on the way home have stopped, and I have heard absolutely nothing more from Habicht. I was pleased to learn from Besso that you successfully finished your examination. It is to be hoped that this will mean a more comfortable material existence for you.

My cordial regards to you and write soon to,

Yours,

A. Einstein

My wife and Mr. Besso send friendly greetings.

August 15, 1908

Dear Solo,

I offer my heartfelt congratulations on your position. You can not imagine how glad I am to know that you are getting along well.

My very best while vacationing.

Your

Einstein

Mileva and Bubi Einstein also send you cordial greetings.

$B\ 4/0$

Bern Donnerstag.

Lieber Solo!

Ihre Ausreden sind zwar ungemein graziös ausgedrückt aber darum nicht weniger faul. Schlaflose Nächte lassen sich bei uns wahrscheinlich prächtig durchführen, nicht minder gut als die schlaflosen halben Akademienächte, an die ich mich noch mit grossem Vergnügen erinnere. Die Ausreden werden also nicht angenommen, sondern es wird Ihre Zusage mit aller Bestimmtheit erwartet. Herzliche Grüsse von Ihrem A. Einstein.

Berne, Thursday
December 3, 1908

Dear Solo,
Your apologies, though very gracefully tendered, are still bad. Here we can probably spend sleepless nights no less magnificently than the sleepless academic half-nights which I fondly recall. Your excuses are not accepted, but your unqualified acceptance is awaited.
Cordial regards from

Your

A. Einstein

Bern 18 III 09

Lieber Solovine!

Ich freute mich sehr mit
Ihrem freundlichen Gruss.
Gestern kam ein junger Japaner
zu mir, der nach Paris geht. Ich
schickte ihn zu Ihnen, in der
Meinung, dass Sie gewiss Vergnüge
an Ihm haben werden. Wann kommen
Sie endlich nach Bern? Sie glauben
gar nicht, wie oft ich an Sie denke
und wie gern ich Sie wiedersähe.
Grüssen Sie meine Schwester und
Ihren Pauli bestens.
　　Mit freundschaftlichem Gruss
　　　　Ihr A. Einstein.
Meine Frau und Bujo lassen
auch bestens grüssen.

Berne
March 18, 1909

Dear Solovine,
    I was elated over your friendly greeting. Yesterday a young Japanese who is going to Paris came to me. I sent him to you, thinking that you would certainly be glad to meet him. When will you ever come to Berne? You can never imagine how often I think of you and how glad I would be to see you. Cordial greetings from my sister and her Pauli.
    With friendly regards

Your

A. Einstein

My wife and Bujo also send their best greetings.

Lieber Solovine! Ich freue mich sehr darauf, dass wir in Paris herumlungern. Wenn nur der verd. Vortrag nicht wäre, den ich — horribile dictu — französisch halten soll.

Mit den besten Grüssen

Ihr Einstein.

Hofstr. 116.

Zürich.

Hofstr. 116
Zurich
[Spring, 1913]

Dear Solovine,
     I am very glad that we shall be able to stroll around in Paris. If only I did not have to give this lecture which—*horribile dictu*—I must give in French.

With best regards,
Your

A. Einstein

Berlin W 30, den 24. IV. 20.

Lieber Solovine!

Ich freue mich sehr, dass Sie etwas über meine Theorie
schreiben wollen. Ich selbst habe zusammenfassend nur ein klei-
nes Büchlein geschrieben, das ich Ihnen hiemit zusende, sonst
nur Originalabhandlungen, deren Separata leider vergriffen sind.
An Büchern empfehle ich auch für den Ankauf der wissenschaftlichen Bibliotheken Weyl: Raum, Zeit, Materie sowie Schlick:
Raum und Zeit in der Gegenwärtigen Physik (beide bei Verlag
Springer, Berlin), und ausserdem ein bei Teubner verlegtes
Bändchen: Das Relativitätsprinzip, in dessen 3. nächstens er-
scheinender Auflage die wichtigsten Originalabhandlungen über
die allgemeine Relativitätstheorie enthalten sind. Ihr Manuskript will ich gern durchlesen.

Mileva geht es gut; ich bin von ihr geschieden, die
Kinder sind bei ihr in Zürich Gloriastr. 59. Albert hat sich
prächtig entwickelt, der Kleine ist leider etwas kränklich.

Besso ist verschiedentlich in der Welt herumgegondelt,
er ist aber wieder am Patentamt in Bern. Paul Winteler und
meine Schwester leben immer noch vergnügt in Luzern.

Es freut mich sehr, dass ich bei dieser Gelegenheit
wieder von Ihnen gehört habe; ich wünsche Ihnen glückliches
Gelingen Ihres kleinen Unternehmens.

Beste Grüsse von Ihrem
A. Einstein.

W 30
Berlin
April 24, 1920

Dear Solovine,
I am very glad to learn that you intend to write something about my theory. I myself have prepared a summary which I am sending to you; aside from that, I have only the original drafts of essays that are, unfortunately, out of print. Books which I recommend for scientific libraries are Weyl's *Time, Space, Matter* and Schlick's *Space and Time in Physics Today* (both published by Springer, Berlin), along with another volume entitled *The Principle of Relativity* and published by Teubner; the third edition of the latter work, soon to appear, will contain the most important of the original essays on the general theory of relativity. I will be glad to read through your manuscript.

Mileva is in good health; I am separated from her; the children are with her in Zurich, Gloriastr. 59. Albert is quite robust; the little one is unfortunately rather sickly.

Besso has roamed through different countries of the world but is again at the Patent Office in Berne. Paul Winteler and my sister are still living happily in Lucerne.

I am very glad to have heard from you again on this occasion; I wish you success in your undertaking.

Best regards from your

A. Einstein

Inhalt und Methode der Relativitätstheorie lässt sich trotz der Mannigfaltigkeit der physikalischen Erfahrungsthatsachen, auf die sie sich
mündet, in wenigen Worten charakterisieren. Im Gegensatz zu der seit dem
Altertum bekannten Thatsache, dass Bewegung nur als relative
Bewegung wahrnehmbar ist, war die Physik auf den Begriff der
absoluten Bewegung gegründet. Die Optik hatte vorausgesetzt, dass
in der Welt einen vor allen ausgezeichneten Bewegungszustand
'e, nämlich denjenigen des Lichtäthers. Auf den Lichtäther wären
: Bewegungen körperlicher Objekte zu beziehen; der Lichtäther
'bst erscheint so als eine Verkörperung des am Ziele leeren Begriffes
absoluter Ruhe. Existierte ein körperlicher Lichtäther, so könnten
: Bewegungen der körperlichen Objekte auf ihn bezogen werden, und
es könnte in diesem physikalischen Sinne von „absoluter Bewegung"
reden und auf diesen Begriff auch die Mechanik gründen. Nachdem alle die Bemühungen gescheitert waren, den durch den
Lichtäther bevorzugten Bewegungszustand durch physikalische
nach aufzufinden, lag es nahe, das Problem umzukehren. Das
ist die Relativitätstheorie in systematischer Weise. Sie setzt
voraus, dass es physikalisch bevorzugte Bewegungs-
zustände in der Natur nicht gebe und fragt nach den Folgerungen,
die aus dieser Voraussetzung bezüglich der Naturgesetze gezogen
den können. Die Methode der Relativitätstheorie ist derjenigen der Thermodyn-
mik weitgehend analog; denn diese letztere Wissenschaft ist insofern
die als die Beantwortung der Frage: Wie müssen die Naturgesetze
schaffen sein, damit es unmöglich ist, ein perpetuum mobile
konstruieren?

[Undated]

The contents and method of the theory of relativity can, despite the variety of experimental physical facts on which the theory is based, be outlined in a few words. In contrast to the fact, known since ancient times, that movement is perceptible only as *relative* movement, physics was based on the notion of *absolute* movement. Optics had assumed that one state of movement, luminous ether, is distinct from all others. All movements of bodies were supposed to be related to the luminous ether, which was the incarnation of absolute motionlessness. If a fixed formal luminous ether filled everything in space, then the movements of bodies would be related to it and one could in this physical sense speak of "absolute movement" and ground mechanics on this notion. But after efforts to discover the privileged state of movement of this hypothetical luminous ether through physical experiments had failed, it seemed that the problem should be restated. That is what the theory of relativity did systematically. It assumed that there are no privileged physical states of movement and asked what consequences could be drawn from this supposition concerning the laws of nature. The method of the theory of relativity is analogous to the method of thermodynamics; for the latter is nothing more than the systematic answer to the question: how must the laws of nature be constructed in order to rule out the possibility of bringing about perpetual motion?

Charakteristisch für die Relativitätstheorie ist ferner ein
der erkenntnistheoretischer Gesichtspunkt. Es gibt in der Physik
keinen Begriff, dessen Verwendung a priori nötig oder berechtigt wäre. Ein
Begriff erhält seine Daseinsberechtigung nur durch seine klare und
eindeutige Verknüpfung mit Erlebnissen bezw. mit physikalischen
~~... ...~~ So wurden in der Relativitätstheorie die Begriffe
absolute Gleichzeitigkeit, absolute Geschwindigkeit, absolute Beschleunigung
verworfen, weil sich ihre eindeutige Verbindung mit der Erlebniswelt
unmöglich herausstellt. Dasselbe Schicksal traf die Begriffe "Ebene"
"Linie" etc, auf welche die euklidische Geometrie gegründet ist. Jeden
~~... ...~~ muss eine solche Definition gegeben werden, dass auf Grund dieser
... das Zutreffen oder nicht Zutreffen desselben im konkreten
... prinzipiell entschieden werden kann.

A further characteristic of the theory of relativity is an epistemological point of view. In physics no concept is necessary or justifiable on an *a priori* basis. A concept acquires a right to existence solely through its obvious and unequivocal place in a chain of events relating to physical experiences. That is why the theory of relativity rejects concepts of absolute simultaneity, absolute speed, absolute acceleration, etc.; they can have no unequivocal link with experiences. Similarly, the notions of "plane," and "straight line," and the like, which form the basis of Euclidian geometry, had to be discarded. Every physical concept must be defined in such a way that it can be used to determine in principle whether or not it fits the concrete case.

Gegen die Auffassung von der räumlich - unendlichen und für die Auffassung einer räumlich - geschlossenen Welt lässt sich also folgendes ausführen:

1) Vom Standpunkt der Relativitätstheorie ist die Bedingung der räumlichen Geschlossenheit viel einfacher als die der quasi-euklidischen Struktur entsprechenden Grenzbedingung im Unendlichen.

2) Der Gedanke Machs, dass die Trägheit auf Wechselwirkungen der Körper beruhe, ist in erster Näherung in den Gleichungen der Relativitätstheorie enthalten; aus ihnen folgt nämlich, dass die Trägheit mindestens zum Teil auf Wechselwirkung der Massen beruht. Es gewinnt dadurch der Mach'sche Gedanke sehr an Wahrscheinlichkeit, da die Annahme unbefriedigend ist, dass die Trägheit zum Teil auf Wechselwirkung, zum Teil auf selbständigen Qualitäten des Raumes beruhe. Dem Mach'schen Gedanken entspricht aber nur eine räumlich geschlossene (endliche) Welt, nicht eine quasi-euklidische, unendliche. Ueberhaupt ist es erkenntnistheoretisch befriedigender, wenn die mechanischen Eigenschaften des Raumes vollständig durch die Materie bestimmt werden, was nur im Falle einer räumlich geschlossenen Welt der Fall ist.

3) Eine unendliche Welt ist nur möglich, wenn die mittlere Dichte der Materie in der Welt verschwindet. Eine solche Annahme ist zwar logisch möglich, aber weniger wahrscheinlich als die Annahme, dass es eine endliche mittlere Dichte der Materie in der Welt gebe.

———————

Against the concept of an infinite spatial world and in favor of a finite spatial world, this much can be said:

(1) From the point of view of the theory of relativity, it is much simpler to conceive of a finite spatial world than a quasi-Euclidian world bounded by infinite space.

(2) Mach's supposition that inertia depends on the reciprocal action of bodies is approximated in the equations of the theory of relativity; from these equations it follows that inertia depends, partly at least, on the reciprocal action of masses. Mach's supposition is therefore well founded, for it is hardly appropriate to suppose that inertia depends partly on reciprocal action and partly on the independent properties of space. But Mach's supposition calls for a finite spatial world, not a quasi-Euclidian infinite world. In short, from the epistemological point of view it is better to have the mechanical properties of space wholly determined by matter, and this obtains only if the world is spatially finite.

(3) An infinite world is possible only if the average density of its matter is lost. Such a supposition is logically possible, to be sure, but it is less probable than the supposition that the world's matter has an average finite density.

Besten Dank für Ihre freundlichen Nachrichten
...en Sie aber auch die 10% pro Exemplar, die
. Ihnen zugedacht habe? Wenn Sie das nicht
...en erwirken können, so behalten Sie einfach
dritten Teil des mir zukommenden Betrages
(den 20%). Ich sehe aus Ihrem Auftrage, ...
...schaft die ... Übersetzung gemacht haben. Ich ver-
...he Ihnen also hiermit noch ausdrücklich das
...setzungsrecht und verspreche Ihnen, dass ich
...en immer zur Übersetzung zur Verfügung stelle,
...sich auf französisch herausgeben will. Wie-
...t kommen auch mathematische Dinge in
...tracht? Mit dem Vertrag bin ich einverstanden.
  Der verd. X.............. hat einfach mein Vorwort
...älscht, indem er –ohne mich zu fragen, Briefe
...nicht einmal direkt von mir stammten, son-
...e von einem Bekannten von mir mit französischer
...igkeit bewässert worden waren, zu einem Vorwort
...dokterte. Wenn Sie mir helfen können, das
...jekt an den Pranger zu stellen, erweisen Sie
...e einen sehr grossen Dienst. Sie erhalten bald
...eine kleine Akademierede nebst Nachtrag zur
...setzung. Was müssen Sie von mir denken, wenn
...solchen Mist zur Übersetzung von mir kriegen-
...übrigens würde ich doch die Akademie fragen müssen
...leicht erlauben dass Chancondsten nicht die
Blokation auf französisch.
...h habe das Buch von X...... überhaupt nicht gelesen
...weiss also nicht, ob es was taugt:

March 8, 1921

Dear Solovine,

Thank you for the cheerful report. But are you collecting the 10% per copy which I had intended for you? If not, then simply keep for yourself one-third of the sum (20%) due me. I can tell by your question that you have been very conscientious about the translation. For that reason I am writing to offer you the exclusive translation right and promise always to place at your disposal whatever I decide to have translated into French. Just how do mathematical writings fit into the picture? I approve of the contract.

That abominable X... falsified my foreword by inserting letters—without my permission—which came, not directly from me, but from an acquaintance of mine whom he had showered with French comeliness. You would be rendering me a great service if you could help me expose the blackguard publicly.* Soon you will receive a short lecture and supplement to be translated. You may be surprised to learn that I have to ask the Academy for permission to have it translated. Perhaps those chauvinists will allow me to publish this nonsense in French.

---

*I have not read the book by X... and therefore do not know whether it has any merit.

Ich gehe gar nicht gern nach Amerika, sondern
thue es nur im Interesse der Zionisten, die für die
Bildungsanstalten in Jerusalem Dollars betteln müssen,
wobei ich als Renommierbonze und Lockvogel dienen
muss. Wenn wir einigermassen auswechselbar
wären, würde ich Sie gerne an meiner Statt gehen lassen.
Aber andererseits thue ich, was ich nur kann, für meine
Stammesbrüder, die überall so gemein behandelt werden.
Ich glaube überhaupt, dass wir uns sehr gut verstehen
werden, wenn wir uns wieder treffen. Ich glaube nicht,
dass mir der viele unverdiente Weihrauch die Seele
geschwärzt hat. Es thut mir leid, dass ich Ihnen
nicht auch wieder Büchlein zum Übersetzen gegeben
habe. Aber wie hätte ich es machen sollen? Wenn
ich zur Abführung des gemeinen X . . . . irgend etwas
~~thun~~ kann, thue ich's sehr gerne. Schreiben Sie mir hierher.
Ich lasse mir's nachsenden, wenn es noch rentiert. Ich
rede am 21. März von hier ab in der Leidener Rede lassen
Sie wohl das Anreden weg — machen Sie's wie Sie es
gut fanden.

         Es grüsst Sie herzlich
            Ihr A. Einstein.

I am not eager to go to America but am doing it solely in the interest of the Zionists, who must beg for dollars to build educational institutions in Jerusalem, and for whom I act as high priest and decoy. If we were at all interchangeable, I would gladly send you in my place. But I am really doing whatever I can for the brothers of my race who are treated so badly everywhere. I am sure that we would understand each other perfectly if we met again. I do not think that all this undeserved incense has blackened my soul. I regret that I failed to give you my little book to translate too. But how could I have done so? If I could do something to put that wretched X... in his place, I would not hesitate. Write me here. Perhaps it is still possible, before the trip. If necessary, I will have it forwarded. I am leaving here on March 21. Leave out the titles of the Leyde lectures—just do whatever you think best.

Most cordial greetings,
Your

A. Einstein

16.<u>IV</u>.21.

Lieber Solovine!

(Gauthier-Villars)

Ich schicke Ihnen die Verträge
unterzeichnet zurück. Die Gelder
bitte ich Herrn Prof. Ehrenfest, Witte
Rooyen Str. Leiden zu senden
mit dem Vermerk, dass sie für
mich bestimmt sind. Dies geschieht,
weil ich viel Geld im Ausland,
bes. in Holland (Branche, und Schweiz)
es so am einfachsten ist. Die Erlaub-
nis von der Akademie habe ich.
Ich reise schon am Samstag ab,
sodass mich keiner Ihrer Briefe
mehr hier erreicht. In zwei Monaten
hoffe ich wieder hier zu sein. Wenn
ich wissenschaftliche Vorträge halte,
so geschieht dies wahrscheinlich
an der Princeton - Universität,

March 16, 1921

Dear Solovine,

I am returning the signed contracts (Gauthier-Villars) to you. Please send the money to Professor Ehrenfest, Witte Rozenstr., Leyde, and indicate that it is for me. I am doing this because I need a considerable amount of money in other countries, especially in Holland and Switzerland, and this arrangement simplifies matters. I have the permission of the Academy. I am leaving this Sunday, with the result that none of your letters will reach me here. In two months I hope to be back here. If I give any lectures in science, it will probably be at Princeton University, where I was first

die mich zuerst eingeladen hat.
Wenn Sie mir nach Amerika
schreiben wollen, so erreicht mich
ein Brief an das Bankhaus
Kuhn Löb, New York.

L. Solovine! Ich bin auch kein
Vaterländer und glaube zuversicht-
lich, dass die Juden durch die
Kleinheit und Abhängigkeit
ihrer Palästina-Kolonie vom Macht-
koller zurückgehalten werden.

L. Solovine, ich plauderte gern
mehr mit Ihnen, aber ich bin
gehetzt wie ein Hase und muss
Minuten schinden. Seien Sie
einstweilen herzlich gegrüsst
von Ihrem
A. Einstein.

invited. If you wish to send letters to me in America, please address them to the Kuhn Loeb Bank in New York.

Dear Solovine! Neither am I a flagwaver, and I believe firmly that the Jews, considering the smallness and dependency of their colony in Palestine, are not threatened by the folly of power.

Dear Solovine! I would like to talk longer with you, but I am like a hare at bay and must use the minutes sparingly. Meanwhile, I send you my cordial regards.

Your

A. Einstein

19. IX. 21.

Lieber Solovine!

Besten Dank für den famosen Artikel und Ihren Vorschlag. Ich kann aber von mir aus nicht in der Zeitung schreiben. Dies verstösst gegen meine geheiligsten Prinzipien und Gewohnheiten. Nur auf Anfrage hin könnte ich mich äussern, wozu es aber zu spät ist, da ich übermorgen abreise. Übrigens haben Sie noch nicht recht verstanden. Ich habe kein Vorwort zu dem X.. geschrieben, sondern er hat es gefälscht, wobei er allerdings unter anderem einige Sätze aus einem Brief von mir benutzt hat. Es wäre mir sehr recht, wenn dieser Sachverhalt bekannt würde.

Es grüsst Sie bestens
Ihr
A. Einstein

March 19, 1921

Dear Solovine,

Many thanks for the splendid article and your proposal. But I myself can not write for a newspaper. That is against my most cherished principles and practices. I could express my opinion only if someone asked me a question, but that is now too late, for I am leaving the day after tomorrow. Besides, you misunderstood me. I wrote *no* foreword for X..., *but he committed a forgery*, using among other things, of course, some sentences from one of my letters. I would be pleased to have this circumstance known.

With warmest regards to you,

Your
A. Einstein

Berlin W. 30, den 14. I. 22
Haberlandstr. 5.

Lieber Solovine!

Viele Arbeit und der Horror gegen das Bücherschreiben machen es mir unmöglich, das Gewünschte zu schreiben. In Bälde bekommen Sie meine Princetoner Vorlesungen. Mit der Edition muss aber gewartet werden bis dieselben in Amerika erschienen sind. Bedingung für den Verleger : 20% des Verkaufspreises, davon bekommen Sie 5%, ich den Rest.

Mit herzlichen Grüssen
Ihr

A. Einstein.

P. S. Frau Untermyer schreiben Sie am besten englisch, damit sie sieht, dass Sie es können. Sie müssen ihr aber auch sagen, dass Sie noch besser deutsch und französisch können. Sie müssen ihr auch sagen, dass wir als junge Männer viel Zeit zusammen verbracht und Studien zusammen betrieben haben. Selbstbewusstes Auftreten in Amerika überall erforderlich, sonst kriegt man nirgends bezahlt und wird gering eingeschätzt.

Berlin
January 14, 1922

Dear Solovine,
   Much work and the horror of writing books make it impossible for me to write what you wish. Soon you will receive my Princeton lectures. They can not be published, however, until they have appeared in America. Terms to the publisher are 20% of the selling price, of which you will receive 5% and I the rest.

With cordial regards
Your

A. Einstein

   It would be better for you to write to Mrs. Untermayer in English to show her that you know the language. But you should also let her know that you understand German and French better. You should also tell her that, when we were youngsters, we stayed side by side for a long time and studied together. A firm approach is indispensable everywhere in America; otherwise one receives no pay and little esteem.

Berlin W.30, den 14. März 1922
Haberlandstr. 5.

Lieber Solovine!

Auf frohes Wiedersehen in Paris! Ich komme dort am 27. oder 28. März an. Langevin besorgt mir einen Unterschlupf, den er Ihnen verraten wird, den ich Sie aber <u>streng geheim zu halten</u> bitte; denn auch so werden die Tage des Pariser Aufenthaltes sehr anstrengend werden.

An dem Vertragsentwurf von Gauthier-Villars habe ich zwei Aussetzungen:

1) Der von mir mit b bezeichnete Absatz muss gestrichen werden, da ich ihm natürlich nur das Verlagsrecht für die französische Uebersetzung geben will.

2) Der mit a bezeichnete Absatz ist mir unverständlich.

Wir können die Angelegenheit vielleicht bei meiner Anwesenheit in Paris erledigen. Ich freue mich sehr auf unser Beisammensein, wenn nur mein Schnabel besser französisch gewetzt wäre.

Mit freundlichen Grüssen
Ihr
A. Einstein.

Berlin W. 30
Haberlandstr. 5
March 14, 1922

Dear Solovine,

How glad I will be to see you again in Paris! I am to arrive on March 27 or 28. Langevin has made arrangements for a hideout, but I beg you *to keep it a deep secret*, for the days that I spend in Paris are going to be very trying.

Concerning the provisional contract with Gauthier-Villars, I have two reservations:

(1) The paragraph which I designated as *b* must be deleted since I am naturally giving him only the French publishing rights.

(2) The paragraph marked *a* makes no sense to me.

Perhaps we can settle the matter during my stay in Paris.

I am very glad that we are going to be together. I only wish I had a better tongue for French.

With friendly regards
Your

A. Einstein

Mr. M. Solovine
B.. de Port-Royal 39
Paris (13ᵉ)

C 154
(10.16)

Lieber Solo

Ich komme am 28 Abends mit dem einzigen in Betracht kommenden Zuge an, allenfalls am Morgen des 29., wenn ich unterwegs den Anschluss verpasse. Hab alles möglichst schon ab- gewimmelt, dass wir etwas Zeit zum Existieren haben

Auf frohes Wiedersehen

Ihr A. Einstein.

Berlin
March 22, 1922

Dear Solo,

I expect to arrive the evening of the 28th on the only evening train or the morning of the 29th at the latest if I miss a connection along the way. I have already gotten rid of everything possible in order to have some time for living.

Looking forward to seeing you, I am

Yours

A. Einstein

20. IV. 22

Lieber Solovine!

Ich danke Ihnen herzlich für die Übersendung der Dinge, die ich in Paris liegen gelassen habe. Es waren unvergessliche Tage, aber verflucht anstrengend; sie stecken mir immer noch in den Nerven. Hier habe ich noch niemand gesehen, aber die Zeitungen verhalten sich durchaus gut, wie man mir sagte, sodass das ganze Unternehmen seinen Zweck erfüllt hat. Die Korrekturen sind noch nicht fertig. Sie werden sie aber erhalten. Der [illegible]-Prozess ist erfolgreich verlaufen; es ist gut, dass ich da war. Ich sende Ihnen einen Brief für Baron Rothschild, den ich weiterzugeben bitte. Hoffentlich werden wir einmal eine Zeit zusammen verbringen mehr im alten Berner Stil.

Herzliche Grüsse von Ihrem

A. Einstein.

April 20, 1922

Dear Solovine,

Hearty thanks for having sent me the things that I left in Paris. Those days were unforgettable but devilishly tiring; my nerves still remind me of them. Here I have not yet seen anyone, but I am told that the newspapers did a good job, with the result that the aim of the operation was fully realized. The corrections have not been completed, but you will receive them. The initial operation was successful; it is good that I was there. I am sending you a letter for Baron Rothschild which I would like for you to give him. Let us hope that we may again spend a day together just as we used to in Berne.

Cordial greetings
Your

A. Einstein

16. XII. 22.

Lieber Solo!

Anbei die Verträge. Die kleinen Abänderungen werde ich am Büchlein anbringen, ebenso an Beck schreiben. Ich freue mich, dass Sie nun zu Ihrer Reise kommen und endlich Ihre Mutter wiedersehen. Hier sind arge Zeiten seit dem unbeschreiblichen Mord an Rathenau. Ich werde noch immer gewarnt, habe mein Kolleg aufgegeben und bin offiziell abwesend, aber in Wahrheit doch hier. Der Antisemitismus ist sehr gross. Die endlosen Chikanen der Entente werden letzten Endes wieder die ... Juden treffen. Man klagt über grosse Chikanen gegen die Industrie, Zerstörungen von Fabrikationsanlagen unter dem Deckmantel der militärischen Brauchbarkeit.

Herzliche Grüsse und viel Vergnügen

Ihr
A. Einstein.

Der Painlevé ist interessant, aber das über Relativität Gesagte dürfte sich schwer halten lassen.

July 16, 1922

Dear Solovine,

Included herewith are the lectures. I shall make the minor changes in the book and correct the mistakes in spelling. I am glad that you are ready to take a trip to see your mother again at last. Here our daily lives have been nerve-racking since the shameful assassination of Rathenau. I am always on the alert; I have stopped my lectures and am officially absent, though I am actually here all the time. Anti-Semitism is strong. The endless chicanery of the Entente will fall upon the Jews again. There are complaints about numberless acts of chicanery against industry, the destruction of factories, under the pretext of military expediency.

Cordial greetings and much happiness
Your

A. Einstein

Painlevé is interesting, but it would be hard to defend what he has to say about relativity.

Pfingsten. 1923.

Lieber Solovine!

In Japan war es wundervoll. Feine Lebensform,
lebendiges Interesse für alles, Kunstsinn, intellektuelle
Nasürdorf bei gutem Verstand — ein feines Volk in einem
malerischen Land. Die Stammesbrüder in Palästina haben
mir sehr gefallen, als Bauern, als Arbeiter und als Bürger.
Das Land ist im Ganzen wenig fruchtbar. Es wird
ein moralisches Zentrum werden, aber keinen grossen
Teil des jüdischen Volkes aufnehmen können. Andrer-
seits bin ich aber überzeugt, dass die Kolonisation gelingen
wird. Ich freue mich, dass Ihre Reise so wohlgelungen
ist. Hoffentlich gibt es sich, dass wir einmal gemütlich
darüber plaudern können. Schicken Sie die Sache von G. W.
Herrn Kuno Kochertthaler, Calle Lealtad, Madrid und nehmen
Sie sich ein Zehntel davon zum Gruss. Ich habe Nordmanns
Adresse nicht, sende Ihnen also die Korrektur zurück.
Die daran geübte Kritik ist leider sehr berechtigt. Er
soll es verbessern. Grüssen Sie ihn freundlich. Ich bin
aus einer Völkerbundskommission ausgetreten, weil ich zu
dieser Institution kein Vertrauen mehr habe. Das hat mir
grimmiges Odium eingetragen, aber ich bin doch froh,
es getan zu haben. Man muss sich vor verlogenen
Unternehmungen fernhalten, auch wenn sie einen
schönen Namen haben. Bergson hat in seinem Buch
über Rel. Theorie schwere Böcke geschossen; Gott wird's ihm
vergeben.

    Herzliche Grüsse von Ihrem

       A. Einstein.

[Pentecost, 1923]

Dear Solovine,

It was wonderful in Japan. Genteel manners, a lively interest in everything, an artistic sense, intellectual honesty together with common sense. The brothers of our race in Palestine charmed me as farmers, as workers and as citizens. The country as a whole is not very fertile. It will become an ethical center but cannot accommodate a very large segment of the Jewish people. But I am convinced that colonization will be successful. I am glad that your trip was such a great success. Let us hope that we can talk about it at our ease one of these days. Send G.V.'s thing to Mr. Kuno Kochenthaler, Calle Lealtad, Madrid, and keep one-tenth for your services. Since I do not have Nordmann's address, I am returning the proof to you. Unfortunately, the criticism leveled at it is justified. He must set it straight. Give him my cordial greetings. I resigned from a commission of the League of Nations, for I no longer have any confidence in this institution. That provoked some animosity, but I am glad that I did it. One must shy away from deceptive undertakings, even when they bear a high-sounding name. Bergson, in his book on the theory of relativity, made some serious blunders; may God forgive him.

Affectionate regards from
Your

A. Einstein

26 VIII

Lieber Solo!

Sie brauchen mir
keine Korrektur zu senden.
Gauthier Vill. kann das
Geld einfach an meine
Berliner Adresse senden
(Haberlandstr. 5)

Herzliche Grüsse von Deinem

A. Einstein

August 26, 1924

Dear Solo,
   You do not have to send the proofs to me. Gauthier-Villars can simply send me the money at my Berlin address (Haberlandstr. 5).

Cordial regards,

A. Einstein

30.X.24,

Lieber Solovine!

Sie erhalten das Heftchen aus
den Klass d. ex. W. und das . . . . .
. . . . Buch von A. M. per Post. Damit
genug des Biographischen. Das Interesse
für Philosophie war bei mir immer
da, aber nur sekundär. Das Interesse
für Naturwissenschaft beschränkte
sich immer in der Hauptsache auf
das Prinzipielle, woraus mein Tun
und Unterlassen am besten verständlich
wird. Dass ich so wenig publiziert habe,
hängt mit dem gleichen Umstand
zusammen, indem die Sehnsucht
nach dem Erfassen des Prinzipiellen
zur Folge hatte, dass die meiste Zeit
auf erfolglose Bemühungen
verwandt wurde. — Die Albertuna-Commer.
war besser, als ich dachte. Es ist doch Hoffnung,
dass es besser wird mit Europa.
Herzliche Grüsse von Ihrem
A. Einstein.

October 30, 1924

Dear Solovine,
You will receive by mail the brochure of Klass. d. ex. W. and the book...by A.M. That should be enough biographical material. I was always interested in philosophy but only as a sideline. My interest in science was always essentially limited to the study of principles, which best explains my conduct in its entirety. That I have published so little is attributable to the same circumstance, for the burning desire to grasp principles has caused me to spend most of my time on fruitless endeavors. The commission of the League of Nations was better than I thought. There is still hope that things will be better in Europe.

Cordial greetings from
Your

A. Einstein

8. XI 29.

Lieber Solo!

Ich will heut über meine neue Theorie vortragen, um 5ʰ 30 im Inst H. Poincaré. Dazu sende ich Ihnen die beiliegende Karte. Den Abend könnten wir dann zusammen sein, wenn Sie Zeit haben. Holen Sie mich nach dem Vortrag.

Auf Wiedersehen

Ihr

A. Einstein.

November 8, 1929

Dear Solo,
     Today I am giving a lecture on my new theory at
5:30 at the H. Poincaré Institute. I am sending you the
enclosed ticket. We can spend the evening together if
you have the time.
     Looking forward to seeing you again, I am

                                        Your

                                        A. Einstein

Mr. Solovine
Boul. Port Royal 39
Paris

Alpenhotel Schönblick, 1400 m.
b. Oberstdorf, b. Allgäu

Nr. 2405

Lieber Solo!

Ich habe Deinen Demokrit sehr gesucht und nicht gefunden, trotzdem ich mich erinnere, ihn von Dir erhalten zu haben. Kannst Du ihn mir noch einmal senden? Ich werde ihn dann sofort lesen und Dir darüber schreiben.

Herzliche Grüße
Dein A. E.

December 28, 1929

Dear Solo,
   I have looked everywhere for your Democritus but have not found it, though I recall having received it from you. Can you send it to me again? I will then read it immediately and write to you about it.

Affectionate regards

A. E.

4. III. 30.

Lieber Solovine!

Es hat ein bischen gedauert, bis ich Ihren Demokrit fertig gelesen habe, weil ich von eigener Arbeit besessen und auch sonst viel abgehalten war. Das alte Exemplar hat sich übrigens unterdessen wiedergefunden.

Am meisten Freude hatte ich an Ihrer Einleitung. Die Darstellung der Beziehung Demokrits zu seinen Vorgängern scheint mir sehr gelungen zu sein. Mir wenigstens ist eine Laterne aufgegangen (Versöhnung des starren Absoluten mit dem formlosen Sichverändern in Atom und Bewegung). Bewundernswürdig am Original ist die Behandlung der Sinnesqualitäten. Rührend, wie er sich mit dem Gesichtssinn plagt, zäh festhaltend an dem Grundgedanken. Unter den moralischen Aphorismen sind einige wirklich gute, aber vieles merkwürdig spiessbürgerlich (Sauherden- Moral - Theorie). Die Übersetzung scheint im Ganzen wirklich gelungen zu sein, soweit ich es mit meinem mangelhaften Französisch beurteilen kann. Bewunderns- wert ist der feste Glaube an die physische Kausalität, die auch vor dem Willen des homo sapiens nicht Halt macht. So viel ich weiss, ist erst Spinoza wieder so radikal und konsequent gewesen.

March 4, 1930

Dear Solovine,

I needed some time to read through your Democritus, for I was burdened down with my own work and disturbed by other things. The first copy turned up in the interval.

I was elated on reading your Introduction. It seems to me that you handled Democritus' relationship to his predecessors beautifully. To me at least it cast new light on one point: the reconciliation of the fixed absolute and formless change (atom and movement). Worthy of admiration in the original is the treatment of perceptible qualities. He goes to great lengths to defend his basic idea in his discussion of the sense of sight. A number of his moral aphorisms have real beauty, but many reek of philistine pettiness (ethical theory of herds of swine). The translation seems on the whole to be letter-perfect insofar as I can judge from my inadequate knowledge of French. Noteworthy is the firm belief in physical causality, which is not even stopped by the will of *Homo sapiens*. To my knowledge only Spinoza was so radical and so consistent.

Meine Feldtheorie macht gute Fortschritte. Cartan hat schon darin gearbeitet. Ich selbst arbeite mit einem Mathematiker (S. Mayer aus Wien), einem prächtigen Kerl, der längst eine Professur hätte, wenn er nicht Jude wäre. Ich denke noch oft an die schönen Tage in Paris, bin aber doch froher mit meiner verhältnismässig ruhigen hiesigen Existenz. Verfügen Sie über mich, wenn Sie denken, dass ich irgend etwas Ihnen kann, was Sie wünschen und seien Sie herzlich gegrüsst von Ihrem

A. Einstein

My field theory is progressing smoothly. Cartan has done some good work in this area. I myself am working with a mathematician (W. Mayer of Vienna), a splendid fellow who would have been given a professorship long ago if he were not a Jew. I often think of the lovely Parisian days, but am satisfied with my relatively peaceful existence here. Do not hesitate to call on me if you think I can be of help in any way.

Cordial regards

A. Einstein

Caputh bei Potsdam, den 6. Juli 1932

Lieber Solovine!

Anbei das Vertragsexemplar mit herzlichem Dank für
Ihren Brief. Die kurze Darlegung über das kosmologische
Problem hoffe ich bald zu schreiben.

Bei dem Kongress in Genf werde ich nicht anwesend sein.
Es genügt, wenn ich im Comité bin. Ich kann vom Schreibtisch
aus mehr nützen als durch persönliche Beteiligung, zumal ich
kein Redner bin.

Herzlich grüsst Sie
Ihr
A. Einstein.

Caputh near Potsdam
July 6, 1932

Dear Solovine,

Herewith the contract with my sincere thanks for your letter. Soon I hope to write the short treatise on the cosmological problem.

I shall not be present at the Geneva congress. It is enough for me to serve on a committee. I can be more useful at my desk than through direct participation, especially so in view of the fact that I am no orator.

Cordial regards to you.
Your

A. Einstein

Caputh bei Potsdam, den 29. IX 32.

Lieber Solo!

Sie Schurke, Sie ungeduldiger! Ich hab das Ding doch erst zusammen schwitzen müssen, neben vieler sonstiger Plackerei und auch wirklicher Arbeit. Nun aber ist es hübsch klar herausgekommen. Hoffentlich gefällt es Ihnen. Ich behalte mir aber vor, das Ding später auch einer englischen Publikation einzuverleiben, die ich schuldig bin seit zwei Jahren.

Hoffentlich geht es Ihnen persönlich gut in dieser verrückten Welt, in der man die Soldaterei nicht ausrotten kann dank der Heuchelei der „Gebildeten".

Herzlich grüsst Sie Ihr
A. Einstein.

Senden Sie mir das Manuskript bitte nach Übersetzung zurück.

Caputh near Potsdam
September 29, 1932

Dear Solo,

You impatient scoundrel! I managed to tie the thing together only after putting myself to a great deal of trouble and going through much reshuffling and some real work. But now it is crystal clear. I hope you will like it. But I reserve the right to incorporate it later into an English publication that I have been promising for two years.

I hope that you, personally, are well in this topsy-turvy world in which the hypocrisy of "cultured people" makes it impossible to exterminate militarism.

Cordial greetings from
Your

A. Einstein

Please return the manuscript after you have made the translation.

Caputh bei Potsdam, den 6. Oktober 32

Lieber Solovine!

Leider bin ich Ende Dezember schon in Amerika, so dass wir uns hier nicht werden sehen können. Das Wörtchen "sogenannt" im Titel habe ich deswegen gesetzt, weil der Ausdruck "Kosmologisches Problem" keine gute Bezeichnung des behandelnden Gegenstandes ist. Ich glaube, wir ändern den Titel um in "Ueber die Struktur des Raumes im Grossen". Hoffentlich finden Sie bald wieder Ihren frohen Mut, der immer so solid auf Resignation gegründet war.

Herzlich grüsst Sie
Ihr
A. Einstein.

Caputh near Potsdam
October 6, 1932

Dear Solovine,

By the end of December I shall be in America,
unfortunately, so that we are not going to be able to see
each other here. I inserted the word "so-called" into the
expression "Cosmological Problem" because the title
did not accurately characterize the subject dealt with. I
believe that we can change the title to "On the Structure of Space in General." I hope that you will soon
regain your usual good humor, which has always been
solidly grounded on resignation.

Cordial regards to you
Your

A. Einstein

Caputh bei Potsdam, den 20. November 32

Lieber Solovine!

Ich bin fest davon überzeugt, dass die ganze Sache bei
Ihnen in wirklich guten Händen liegt und ermächtige Sie, alles
ohne mich nach Ihrem Ermessen fertig zu machen. Die Exemplare
schicken Sie am besten erst nächsten April an meine Caputher
Adresse. In Amerika brauche ich sie nicht.

Sagen Sie Herrn Langevin nochmals meinen herzlichsten
Dank und drängen Sie ihn, dass er bald auf meinen Brief ant-
wortet. Es handelt sich nämlich um eine internationale Ver-
einigung von zuverlässig pazifistisch eingestellten führenden
Intellektuellen, welche versuchen sollen, als Gesamtheit durch
die Presse politischen Einfluss in den Fragen der Abrüstung,
Sicherheit etc. zu gewinnen. Langevin müsste die Seele einer
solchen Gemeinschaft sein, weil er nicht nur guten Willen sondern auch viel politisches Verständnis hat.

Herzlich grüsst Sie
Ihr
A. Einstein.

Caputh near Potsdam
November 20, 1932

Dear Solovine,

I am firmly convinced that with you the whole affair is in good hands, and I give you full authority to settle everything without me, using your own judgment. It would be best for you to send the copies to me next April at my Caputh address only. I do not need them in America.

Tell Langevin that I again thank him sincerely, and insist that he answer my letter soon. There is to be an international meeting of distinguished intellectuals who are staunch pacifists; their aim is to gain a voice as a body in the political press and exert their influence on questions of disarmament, security, etc. Langevin should be the soul of such a group, for he has not only good will but also keen political insight.

Cordial greetings,
Your

A. Einstein

Le Coq bei Ostende 23. *IV*. 33.

Lieber Solo!

Ich bin nicht dazu gekommen, Ihren Brief rechtzeitig zu beantworten, so hagelte es Briefe und Menschen! Meine Angst ist, dass diese Hass- und Gewalt-Seuche sich überall ausbreiten wird. Das kommt wie eine Überschwemmung von unten nach oben, bis die oberen isolieren, verängstigt und - demoralisiert sind und auch in der Flut versinken. - Ich hab nun mehr Professoren als verständige Gedanken in meinem Hirn. Der Teufel scheisst auf den grossen Haufen!

Genug von dem Unsinn. Hoffentlich sehen wir uns doch einmal, wenn es ruhiger um mich geworden ist. Einstweilen grüsst Sie herzlich Ihr

A. E.

Wenn Sie jüdische aus Deutschland geflüchtete Akademiker sehen, dann veranlassen Sie sie, sich mit mir in Verbindung zu setzen. Ich möchte mit ein paar Freunden versuchen, eine jüdische Gast-Universität für jüdische Dozenten und Professoren im Ausland (England?) ins Leben zu rufen, um wenigstens den dringendsten Bedürfnissen zu entsprechen und eine Art geistiger Zuflucht zu schaffen.

Le Coq near Ostend
April 23, 1933

Dear Solo,
I could not manage to answer your letter on time,
so great was the stream of letters and men. I fear that
this epidemic of hatred and violence will become
widespread. It rises like a torrent until the upper layers
are isolated, distressed, demoralized and engulfed by
the flood. I now have more professorship than rational
ideas in my head. The devil mocks the people!
Enough nonsense. Let us hope that we may still see
each other one day when calmness has again enfolded
me.
In the meantime I send you my warmest regards.

Your

A. Einstein

If you see any Jewish academicians who are refu-
gees from Germany, please have them get in touch with
me. I would like to try with some friends to found a free
university abroad (England?) for Jewish teachers and
professors; it might at least meet their most pressing
needs and create a sort of intellectual refuge.

Le Coq, den 19. Mai 33

Lieber Solovine,

Mit Pfingsten ist es wieder nichts. Ich muss nämlich übermorgen nach Zürich zu meinem kranken Sohn und dann sofort nach Oxford (Christchurch College), wo ich bis etwa 20. Juni bleiben muss. Es ist wohl möglich, dass ich nachher nach Paris komme im Zusammenhang mit der Angelegenheit vom Collège de France. In diesem Falle sehen wir uns in Paris, andernfalls hoffentlich hier, wo ich den Sommer zu verbleiben gedenke. Trotz aller Aufregungen und Ablenkungen habe ich mit meinem wissenschaftlichen Freunde hier eine schöne Arbeit gemacht, über die ich glücklich bin.

Herzlich grüsst Sie (in Eile)
Ihr
A. Einstein.

Le Coq
May 19, 1933

Dear Solovine,
Nothing again concerning the Pentecost project. As a matter of fact, I have to go to Zurich the day after tomorrow to see my ailing son and immediately thereafter to Oxford (Christ Church College) where I am to remain until about June 20. It is quite possible that I shall then come to Paris for the business of the Collège de France. In that case, we may see each other in Paris; otherwise, I hope it will be here, where I intend to spend the summer. Despite all the excitement and interruptions, I am happy because of the good work which I have done here with my scientist friend.

Warmest greetings to you (hastily),
Your

A. Einstein

Lieber Solovine!

Ich hoffe, dass ich Ihnen noch die Übersetzung unseres Büchleins ins Französische zuwenden kann. Herr Infeld hat zwar bereits einem französischen Verlagsunternehmen das Verlagsrecht zugesichert (Flamarion); wir haben uns aber das Recht vorbehalten, den Übersetzer selber zu wählen. Herr Infeld hat dem Verlag bereits Ihre Adresse geschrieben. Das Buch kam dadurch zustande, dass ich Herrn Infeld, dem ein Stipendium abgeschlagen worden war, einen gesicherten Lebens-Unterhalt verschaffen musste. Wir haben die Sache zusammen recht sorgfältig ausgearbeitet mit besonderer Berücksichtigung des erkenntnistheoretischen Gesichtspunktes. Wie nämlich zu Machs Zeit ein dogmatisch-materialistischer Standpunkt schädlich dauernde, so in unserer Zeit ein übertriebener positivistisch-subjektivistischer. Man erklärt den Anspruch auf Erfassung der Natur als objektiver Realität als veraltetes Vorurteil, indem man aus der Not der Quanten-Theoretiker eine Tugend macht. Die Menschen sind eben suggestibler als die Pferde, und eine Mode beherrscht jede Zeit, ohne dass die meisten den sie beherrschenden Tyrannen auch nur zu sehen bekommen.

Princeton
April 10, 1938

Dear Solovine,

I still hope to be able to entrust the translation of
our book into French to you. Mr. Infeld has, it is true,
already promised a French concern (Flammarion) the
publication rights; but we reserved the right to choose
the translator ourselves. Mr. Infeld has already given
your address to the publisher. The book owes its existence to the fact that I was obliged to provide for Mr.
Infeld, who was refused a fellowship. We worked out
the subject very carefully together, giving particular
attention to the epistemological point of view. In
Mach's time a dogmatic materialistic point of view
exerted a harmful influence over everything; in the
same way today, the subjective and positivistic point of
view exerts too strong an influence. The necessity of
conceiving of nature as an objective reality is said to be
superannuated prejudice while the quanta theoreticians
are vaunted. Men are even more susceptible to suggestion than horses, and each period is dominated by a
mood, with the result that most men fail to see the
tyrant who rules over them.

Wenn es nur in der Wissenschaft so wäre, dann könnte man sich mit einem vergnügten Lächeln begnügen. Aber im politischen Leben ist es noch viel ärger, und das geht uns an den Kragen. Es ist so scheusslich gegenwärtig, dass nicht ein einziger Lichtblick bleibt Bösartige Narren auf einer seite und feige Selbstsucht auf der anderen. Amerika ist natürlich auch nicht anders, aber alles kommt später und langsamer. Sie passen nicht daher. Man muss jung sein und nach einer faden Schablone gemodelt, wenn man nicht verhungern soll. Ich werde allerdings als altes abgestempeltes Museumsstück und Kuriosum hoch geschätzt; aber solches Hobby geht nebenher. Ich arbeite immer noch fest drauf los, unterstützt von einzigen wagemutigen jüngeren Kollegen. Denken kann ich noch, aber die Arbeitskraft hat nachgelassen. Und dann: tot sein ist auch nicht übel.

      Herzlich grüsst Sie Ihr

        A. E.

If this were true only of science, one could dismiss it with a smirk. But the same holds in politics and in our lives. Our times are so wretched that not one enlightened man is left. On the one hand are fools with evil intentions; on the other, a base egotism. Naturally, America is no different, everything coming here later and more slowly. You are not made for this situation. One must be young and cut to a pattern or die of hunger. To be sure, I am highly esteemed, like an old museum piece or curiosity, but such a dada is overlooked. I work earnestly always, supported by a few courageous colleagues. I can still think, but my capacity for work has slackened. And then: to be dead is not so bad after all.

Warmest greetings,
Your

A. E.

Nassau Point, Peconic Long Island, N.Y.
den 27. Juni 1938

Lieber Solovine:

Ich glaube, es wäre vorteilhafter, wenn Sie mit Ihrer Mutter Platz tauschen könnten, wenigstens soweit Valutagründe in Betracht kommen. Die deutsche Uebersetzung ist von einem langweiligen Kollegen gemacht, dem wir dieselbe leider aus Mitleid übertrugen. Halten Sie sich also besser an den englischen Text, wie Sie selbst vorschlagen.

In der englischen Ausgabe ist bei den Ausführungen über die Lichtfortpflanzung leider eine unrichtige Behauptung über die Zeit des Sonnenunterganges. Es ist mir unbegreiflich, wie mein sonst so zuverlässiger Kollege das hat schreiben und wie ich es habe durchgehen lassen können. Es wird dort behauptet, dass im Augenblick der Beobachtung des Sonnenuntergangs die Sonne in Wahrheit schon sechs Minuten untergegangen sei. Dieser Irrtum entspringt einer geozentrischen Darstellung vom Standpunkt eines mit der Erde rotierenden Koordinatensystems. Leider kann ich die Stelle nicht finden, sie wird Ihnen aber schon auffallen. So kann ich im Moment nicht sagen, ob der Satz ohne Schaden weggelassen werden kann oder durch einen anderen zu ersetzen ist.- Die Curricula können Sie weglassen; Korrekturen brauchen Sie nicht zu schicken, ich habe volles Vertrauen auf Ihr Verständnis.

Nassau Point, Peconic
Long Island, N.Y.
June 27, 1938

I believe it would be to your advantage to exchange places with your mother. The German translation was made by an irksome colleague who owes our approval, alas, to pity. You should therefore concentrate your efforts, as you yourself suggest, on the English text.

In the English edition there is unfortunately, with respect to developments concerning the propagation of light, a misstatement of fact as to the time of the setting of the sun. I simply can not understand how my colleague, who can usually be relied on, could have written that or how I could have let it pass. The passage states that at the instant a sunset is observed, the setting has actually occurred six minutes earlier. This mistake springs from a geocentric description from the point of view of a system of coordinates that rotate with the earth. Unfortunately, I cannot find the passage, but you will certainly come across it. Thus I cannot say at the moment whether the sentence should be deleted or replaced by another. You may leave out the *curricula*: you need not send me the proofs; I have full confidence in you intelligence.

Der Titel "Evolution de la Physique" scheint mir die
Absicht nicht ganz wieder zu geben. Ich war auch mit dem
gewählten englischen Titel eigentlich nicht ganz einverstanden. Der deutsche Titel scheint mir zutreffender, weil er das
psychologische, bezw. subjektive Moment in den Vordergrund
stellt. Das Wort "clew" bedeutet in der Detektivsprache einen
entscheidenden Gesichtspunkt ("Spur"), der zur Aufhellung
eines Verbrechens bezw. zu einer kausalen Verbindung der ent-
deckten empirischen Einzeltatsachen führt. Sie werden schon
das richtige französische Wort wählen.- Es ist nicht richtig,
dass ich nach Europa fahre. Ich bleibe hier den Sommer über in
einem stillen Winkel und richte es überhaupt immer so ein, dass
ich möglichst wenig mit Menschen zu tun habe. Wenn einer dies
begreifen kann, dann sind Sie es.

Ich arbeite mit meinen jungen Leuten an einer überaus
interessanten Theorie, mit der ich die gegenwärtige Wahrschein-
lichkeits-Mystik und Abkehr vom Realitätsbegriff auf dem physikalischen Gebiete zu überwinden hoffe. Sprechen Sie aber
nicht darüber, weil ich noch nicht weiss, ob ich damit zu
Ende komme.

Herzlich grüsst Sie
Ihr
A. Einstein

The Title *Evolution de la Physique* does not seem to me to express the intention exactly. Actually, I was not in complete agreement on the English title. The German title seems more apt to me, for it points up the psychological or subjective moment. The word "clue" as used in police jargon means a decisive point of view (trail) that leads to the solution of a crime or to a causal chain of isolated facts revealed by experience. The choice of the right French word is up to you. It is not true that I am leaving for Europe. I am staying here in a quiet corner during the summer and always struggling to have as little as possible to do with others. If anyone can understand this, it would have to be you.

I am working with my young people on an extremely interesting theory with which I hope to defeat modern proponents of mysticism and probability and their aversion to the notion of reality in the domain of physics. But say nothing about it, for I still do not know whether the end is in sight.

Cordial greetings to you
Your

A. Einstein

den 23. Dezember 1938

Lieber Solovine:

Das von Ihnen geschilderte Unglück bezüglich der französischen Ausgabe des Buches mag ja gross sein. Ich denke aber, dass
wir überaus glücklich sein müssen, wenn es das Schlimmste wäre,
was gegenwärtig durch menschliche Schuld sich begibt. Wir wollen
uns also mit Humor ins Unvermeidliche fügen.°

Es ist furchtbar, dass Frankreich Spanien und die Czecho-
Slowackei verraten hat. Das Schlimmste daran ist, dass es sich
bitter rächen wird.

In der wissenschaftlichen Arbeit bin ich auf eine wunder-
bare Arbeit gestossen, an der ich mit zwei jungen Kollegen mit
grossem Eifer arbeite. Es besteht Hoffnung, auf diese Weise die
mir unerträgliche statistische Grundlage der Physik zu überwinden. Es ist eine Erweiterung der allgemeinen Relativitätstheorie
von grosser logischer Einfachheit.

Herzlich grüsst Sie
Ihr
A. Einstein

× Die Exemplare sind angekommen und sehen
sehr hübsch aus. Wann ich Zeit finden werde, mir
den Inneren genauer anzusehen, wissen die Götter

December 23, 1938

Dear Solovine,

The misfortune which you describe concerning the French edition of the book is great. But I think that we should consider ourselves extremely fortunate if this were the worst that actually happens through human frailty. Let us then bow ungrudgingly to the inevitable.*

France's betrayal of Spain and Czechoslovakia is frightful. The worst part is that the consequences will be deplorable.

In my scientific work I have come across a wonderful subject which I am studying enthusiastically with two young colleagues. It offers the possibility of destroying the statistical basis of physics, which I have always found intolerable. This extension of the general theory of relativity is of very great logical simplicity.

Warmest greetings to you,
Your

A. Einstein

---

*The copies arrived and look beautiful. Only the gods know when I shall find time to look more closely at the poor things.

den 29. August 1946

Lieber Solovine:

Ich habe mich sehr gefreut über Ihren Brief und warte un
geduldig darauf, Sie wiederzusehen, nachdem ich - offen gesta
den - sehr besorgt um Sie gewesen war. Sie schreiben mir so
höflich, wie wenn Sie nicht mit mir Schweine gehütet und sons
andere Sachen mit mir getrieben hätten, als wir noch beide ju
waren. Ich hatte auch Nachricht von den Habichts, die Sie wah
scheinlich aus den Augen verloren haben werden.

Herzliche Grüsse an Sie und die Ihren und auf frohes
Wiedersehen im Oktober

Ihr

A. Einstein

August 29, 1946

Dear Solovine,

I was very glad to receive your letter, and can hardly wait to see you again after having been seriously concerned over you, I must confess. You write to me so politely—as if you had never herded pigs with me and done other things with me when we were both still young. I have also heard from Habicht, whose whereabouts are probably unknown to you.

Wishing you and yours the very best and looking forward to our happy reunion in October, I am

Your

A. Einstein

den 5. October 1946

Lieber Solovine:

Ich freue mich sehr auf Sie und dass wir uns in dieser besten aller Welten noch einmal sehen und über alles mögliche disputieren können. Sie wohnen bei mir, erstens sowieso und zweitens weil gegenwärtig kein Zimmer hier zu haben ist. Also los!

Ihr alter

A. Einstein.

October 5, 1946

Dear Solovine,
    I am very happy because of you and because we can see each other once again in this best of all possible worlds and talk about all possible things. You will live with me, first because you should and second because right now it is impossible to find a room here. So there!

Same as ever,
Your

A. Einstein

9.April 47

Lieber Solovine:

Sie wären schon allein imstande, mein schlechtes Gewissen lebendig zu erhalten, wenn es nicht sonst genug Nahrung fände. Denn Sie haben mir wiederholt so lieb und ausführlich geschrieben. Das war ja eine ganz abenteuerliche Rückreise, auf der Sie Onkel Sam gründlich von der Rückseite kennen lernten, indem Sie von der Nähe sahen, wie er mit den Verfolgten umspringt - genauer mit denen, die andere verfolgt haben; er selber leistet auch Manches auf diesem Gebiete und macht darin grosse Fortschritte.

Vom Tode Langevins hatte ich schon erfahren. Er war mir einer der Liebsten, ein wahrer Heiliger und dabei hochbegabt. Es ist wahr, dass die Politiker seine Güte ausgenützt haben, indem er nicht imstande war niedere Motive zu durchschauen, die ihm so fremd waren. - Es ist erstaunlich, dass Frankreich sich so langsam erholt; ich glaube, dass das die Kehrseite ihres Individualismus ist, der verantwortlichen Gemeinsinn nicht aufkommen lässt, wenn nicht auf der Basis nationaler Eitelkeit. Bedanken Sie sich nie mehr für die paar Bissen, die wir Ihnen senden dürfen; das beschämt mich zu sehr. Ihrem Arzte danke ich sehr für seine wohlgemeinten und gewiss sachkundigen Ratschläge. Ich muss aber dafür sorgen, dass ich meine Gesundheit ohne zu viel Lüge als schlecht bezeichnen kann, da dies mein einziger wirksamer Schutz ist. Es hatte sich übrigens herausgestellt, dass ein grosser Teil davon durch zu wenig Essen bedingt war; sie haben mich mit gutem Erfolg wieder zurechtgemästet (Heil Amerika). Ihren Epikur habe ich mit grossem Interesse gelesen. Darin hat er jedenfalls recht, dass Moral nicht auf Glauben, d. h. Aberglauben gegründet werden soll. Auch die eudämonistische Auffassung trifft gewiss in erster Näherung das Richtige. Aber ich fühle doch kräftig, dass diese Auffassung zu primitiv ist. Mit dem guten Handeln ist es wie mit den guten Gedichten. Man spürt es kräftig,

April 9, 1947

Dear Solovine,

You alone would suffice to keep my bad conscience alive if it did not find ample nourishment elsewhere. For you have written me in such an amiable manner and in such detail at different times. You had an adventurous trip and were able to become acquainted with both sides of Uncle Sam; you had a good look at his cavalier treatment of persecuted people, or rather those whom others have persecuted; he is undertaking a number of things in this area and making great progress.

I had already learned of Langevin's death. He was one of my dearest acquaintances, a true saint, and talented besides. True, the politicians exploited his goodness since he was unable to ferret out the base motives which were so foreign to his nature. It is surprising that France is recovering so slowly; I believe that this is the reverse of her individualism, which does not allow responsible public opinion to come to light unless it serves the purpose of national pride. Never thank me again for whatever bits we have the right to send you; it confuses me too much. I thank your doctor profusely for his well intentioned and competent advice, but I must be careful in describing my health, without lying too much, as bad, for this is my only effective weapon. Besides, they have already discovered that it was due largely to a deficient diet; by enriching the diet, they were successful in restoring my good health. I read your Epicurus with intense interest. He is quite right in saying that ethics must not be based on belief, that is, on superstition. The eudemonic concept is certainly fitting. But I feel strongly that it is too primitive. Good acts are like good poetry. They are sensed easily

kann es aber nur ganz unvollkommen rational erfassen. Selbst aber, wenn man die Doktrin annimmt, ist das Gleichheitsgefühl eine prekäre Basis, desto nebliger, je genauer man hinsieht. Haben die geistreichsten Leute sich doch nicht einmal darüber klar werden können, was das Wesen des Witzes und des Humors ist, und worauf sich die starke Wirkung gründet. Meiner Schwester geht es subjektiv gut, aber es ist eine abschüssige Bahn, auf der es kein Zurück gibt. Die Margot ist etwas stärker geneigt, als die der meisten Altersgefährten. Ich lese ihr gegenwärtig abends die Kyropädie von Xenophon vor, ein ganz köstliches Werk. So was Treffendes und Unverkünsteltes haben uns Griechen zustande gebracht. Es ist lieb, dass Sie Frau François eingeladen haben. Für sie gilt Heines schönes Wort: Wenn es Dukaten regnete, würden sie ihr nur Löcher in den Kopf schlagen. Ich plage mich sehr mit der Kreuzigung (oder Fälschigierung) meiner Gleichungen mit meinem Herrn Straus. Wir sind aber weit von einer Überwindung der mathematischen Schwierigkeiten. Es ist ein hartes Geschäft, zu dem ein solider Mathematiker überhaupt die Courage nicht aufbringen würde. Mit dem Buche ist es sehr recht, und ich bin überzeugt, dass Sie es gut korrigiert haben. Wo die blöde Stelle mit dem Sonnen-Untergang steht, weiss ich nicht. Der menschliche Sauer freut sich, wenn er so einen Japsen entdeckt, also warum ihm ein Vergnügen wegnehmen (Epikers). Hat letzterer übrigens die Schadenfreude in seine Bilanz aufgenommen. Diese ist nach ihm entschieden als Positivum zu buchen, wenn der Schaden nicht durch Menschen verursacht ist. (Dies nur als Nickerei). Eben sehe ich, dass sie die "Evolution ..." auf Englisch haben wollen, es lohnt nicht wegen des dummen Fehlers etwas zu ruehen. Wahrscheinlich ist es in den späteren englischen Ausgaben auch gar nicht mehr drin.

Alles Gute für Sie beide! Ihr

A. Einstein.

but are only partially understood. Even if the doctrine is accepted, the feeling of goodness is a precarious basis, for the more closely one looks, the more nebulous it becomes. The most ingenious people have not succeeded in determining even the nature of the escape of mind and mood and the basis of their powerful effect. Subjectively my sister feels well, but she is going down a steep grade from which there is no return. Hers is a little steeper than that of most people of the same age. Currently I am reading Xenophon's *Cyropaedia* to her in the evening. It is an exquisite work. Something so fitting and so natural was realized only by the Greeks. It was very kind of you to have invited Mrs. François. Heine's beautiful line applies to her: "If it rained ducats, she would have only holes in her head." In Mr. Straus' company I am always bothered considerably by the verification (or refutation) of my equations. But we are far from having surmounted the mathematical difficulties. It is a hard matter, which even a real mathematician would not have the courage to attack. As for the book, I am convinced that you did a good job in correcting it. I do not know where the ridiculous passage about the sunset is. The reader enjoys discovering such a lapse, so why deprive him of his pleasure (Epicurus). Did the latter have a place for malicious pleasure on his balance sheet? According to him, it would definitely be considered as positive if the injury is not caused by men. (Here I am only kidding.) I surmise that you wish the English *Evolution*.... Sending the stupid thing is not worth the bother. It is probably not obtainable in the latest English editions.

All the best you both!

Your

A. Einstein

den 26. August 1947

Lieber Solovine:

Mir gehts recht gut mit ein bischen auf und ab, und Majas
Zustand ist auch befriedigend (den Umständen gemäss). Ich habe
viel Freude gehabt an der Lektüre Ihres Epicur. Dass der Mann
im Grossen recht hat mit seiner Ethik ist wohl kaum zu bezwei-
feln. Andererseits scheint es mir doch nicht den Gegenstand zu
erschöpfen, weil die als positiv empfundenen Werte bis zu einem gewissen Grade incomensurable sind und nicht so ohne weiteres addiert und subtrahiert werden können. Angenommen z.B.
wir wären überzeugt, dass die Glücksumme bei den Ameisen
günstiger liegt als bei den Menschen, wäre es dann vom ethi-
schen Standpunkte aus richtig, wenn die Menschen den Ameisen
das Feld räumten? Jedenfalls ärgern Sie sich nicht über mich
und meine Hartnäckigkeit und seien Sie versichert, dass wir
es in Bezug auf Hitze und Feuchtigkeit grossartig mit Euch
aufnehmen können.

Mit meinem hauptsächlichen Problem plage ich mich unent-
wegt aber ohne entscheidenden Erfolg.

Mit herzlichen Grüssen von uns Allen an Sie und Ihre Frau
Ihr
A. Einstein.

August 26, 1947

Dear Solovine,

I am getting along well, with a few ups and downs, and so is Maja (all things considered). I was delighted to read your Epicurus. All in all, it would be hard to deny that the man's system of ethics is logical. Against this, it seems to me that he fails to exhaust his subject, for the values shown as positive are to some extent incommensurable and can not without further elaboration be added or subtracted. Suppose, for instance, that we are convinced that the cumulative happiness of ants is higher than that of men. Would it then be right from the ethical point of view for men to surrender to the ants? Regardless, do not lose your temper because of me and my stubbornness, and rest assured that as far as heat and humidity are concerned, we can offer you large-scale competition.

I torment myself bravely with my main problem but without obtaining any decisive result.

With cordial greetings from all of us to you and your wife.

Your

A. Einstein

Lieber Solo!

Der liebe Gott hat es scheints recht gemütlich aufgenommen, was Sie ihm aufgetragen haben. Aber gewirkt hat es doch, wie Sie aus diesem Briefe sehen. Er richtet sich wahrscheinlich gewissenhaft nach der Maxime jenes Ministerialbeamten: Es gibt keine Angelegenheit, die so drängend wäre, dass sie nicht bei längerem Liegenlassen noch drängender werden könnte.

Mein Freund Lowe hat mir von Ihnen erzählt. Aus seinem Berichte geht deutlich hervor, dass es ausser dem oben erwähnten Gott und einigen „Schiebern" in Frankreich niemand mehr gut geht. Umso mehr ist es anzuerkennen, dass man sich dort gegen „unsere" Politik wehrt, die Nazis in Deutschland zu neuer Macht zu bringen, um sie gegen die bösen Russen zu verwenden. Es ist kaum zu glauben, wie wenig die Menschen selbst aus den härtesten Erfahrungen lernen. Ich habe Hadamard auf seine Anregung hin ein Telegramm zur Unterstützung des ~~politischen~~ Widerstandes gegen diese Politik ~~von Seiten~~ geschickt, worin steht: es hätte diesen Weltkrieg nicht gegeben, wenn man auf den weitblickenden Clemenceau gehört hätte. Hoffentlich setzen diese Intellektuellen etwas durch.

Bei uns gehts so weit gut. Auch meine Schwester leidet nicht, obwohl es objektiv betrachtet deutlich abwärts mit ihr geht. Ich lese ihr noch immer jeden Abend vor – heute zum Beispiel die merkwürdigen Argumente, welche Ptolemäus gegen Aristarchs Ansicht vorbringt, dass sich die Erde drehe und sogar um die Sonne bewege. Ich habe dabei an manche Argumente der heutigen Physiker denken müssen: gelehrt und raffiniert, aber instinktlos. Das Abwägen von Argumenten in theoretischen Dingen bleibt eben Sache der Intuition.

Wissenschaftlich bin ich immer noch gehemmt durch dieselben mathematischen Schwierigkeiten, die mir die Bestätigung oder Widerlegung meiner allgemeinen relativistischen Feldtheorie unmöglich machen, trotzdem ich einen sehr tüchtigen jungen Mathematiker zum Mitarbeiter habe. Ich werde es nicht mehr fertig bringen; es wird vergessen werden und muss wohl später wieder entdeckt werden. So ist es ja schon mit so vielen Problemen gegangen.

November 25, 1948

Dear Solo,

The good Lord seems to have been very non-chalant about accepting your consignment, but the effect was still the same, as you see by this letter. He probably follows scrupulously the maxim of a governmental employee: There is no affair so pressing that it will become more pressing if laid aside for some time.

My friend Lowe spoke to me about you. From his account it is clear that aside from the above-mentioned God and some black marketeers, no one in France lives better. It is worth noting also that there are attempts to uphold "our" policy of bringing the Nazis back to power in Germany in order to use them against the wicked Russians. It is hard to believe that men learn so little from their toughest experiences. Following his suggestion, I sent Hadamard a telegram to support opposition to the policy. In it I said: "This world war would not have occurred if people had listened to the far-sighted Clemenceau." Let us hope that the intellectuals will achieve something.

At home, everything goes smoothly so far. My sister does not suffer, though, objectively, she sinks visibly. I always read to her in the evening—today, for instance, the odd arguments which Ptolemy advances against Aristarchus' opinion that the world rotates and even moves around the sun. I could not keep from thinking of certain arguments of present-day physicians: learned and subtle, but without insight. The examining of arguments in theoretical affairs is precisely a matter of intuition.

In my scientific activity, I am always hampered by the same mathematical difficulties, which make it impossible for me to confirm or refute my general rela-

Ich habe bei der Abendlektüre meiner Schwester einiges aus den philosophischen Schriften des Aristoteles vorgelesen. Es war eigentlich recht enttäuschend; wenn es nicht so dunkel und konfus wäre, hätte sich diese Art Philosophie nicht so lange halten können. Aber die meisten Menschen haben eben einen heiligen Respekt vor Worten, die sie nicht begreifen können und betrachten es als Zeichen der Oberflächlichkeit eines Autors, wenn sie ihn so begreifen können. Es ist ein rührendes Zeichen von Bescheidenheit.

Die Engländer zeigen gegen unser jüdisches Volkehre eine Art klinisches Ressentiment, das ich ihnen nicht zugetraut hätte. Aber ihre Politik zuhause ist wirklich anzuerkennen. Vielleicht sind sie die einzigen, die mit dem überalterten Kapitalismus ohne Revolution fertig werden. Objektiv sind sie eigentlich viel schlechter daran als Frankreich, das weder übervölkert ist noch auf Nahrungsimport angewiesen ist.

In den letzten Monaten war ein Sohn von Conrad Habicht hier, ein sehr nettes und gesundes Bürschlein, das nun Mathematiker geworden ist. Vom Alten habe ich bei dieser Gelegenheit auch noch einmal gelebt. Es war doch eine schöne Zeit damals in Bern, als wir unsere lustige „Akademie" betrieben, die doch weniger kindisch war, als jene respektabeln, die ich später von Nähem kennen gelernt habe.

Es ist eine die guten Seiten des Alters, dass man zu allen menschlichen Taten eine wohl-thuende Distanz gewinnt. Sie brauchten allerdings dafür nicht erst alt zu werden!

Herzliche Grüsse und Wünsche von Ihrem

A. E.

tivist field theory, though I have a very competent young mathematician as collaborator. I shall never solve it; it will fall into oblivion and be discovered anew later. That has already happened to many problems.

Among the works that I have been reading to my sister in the evening are certain things from the philosophical writings of Aristotle. They were actually deceptive. If they had not been so obscure and so confusing, this kind of philosophy would not have held its own very long. But most men revere words that they can not understand and consider a writer whom they can understand to be superficial. That is a touching sign of modesty.

The English show a kind of cheap resentment which I would not have believed possible against our small Jewish tribe. But their internal politics really deserves praise. They are perhaps the only ones to end outmoded capitalism without a revolution. Objectively they are actually in a worse condition than France, which is neither overpopulated nor reduced to importing foodstuffs.

During these last months, one of Conrad Habicht's sons came here; he is a very clean-cut, well-built boy, who is also a mathematician. Once again I had news of the old man. We really had a wonderful time in Berne, when we were intent upon our studies in our happy "Academy," which was less childish than the respectable Academies that I became more intimately acquainted with later on.

One of the good sides of old age is in gaining the right perspective for viewing all things human. *You* certainly do not have to grow old for that.

Cordial greetings and wishes from

Your

A. E.

Lido Beach,
Sarasota, Florida
den 22. Februar 1949

Lieber Solovine,

Der von Ihnen erwähnte Briefwechsel mit einem Schulmädchen in Südafrika eignet sich nicht im Geringsten für Ihren Zweck. Es war darin hauptsächlich das Erstaunen ausgedrückt, dass ich nicht schon 300 Jahre tot wäre (Verwechslung mit Newton).

Ich bin hier für drei Wochen in Florida, von jetzt an nur noch 4 Tage. Die Operation war eine Bauchoperation gestützt auf eine nicht ganz zutreffende Vermutung. Ich habe mich gut erholt und die Operation ist nicht vergeblich gewesen, weil einige Verwachsungen korrigiert worden sind. Ich bin aber immer noch geschwächt; viel kann man in diesem Alter nicht mehr erwarten.

Mit herzlichen Grüssen an Sie und Ihre Frau

Ihr

A. Einstein

Lido Beach
Sarasota, Florida
Februrary 22, 1949

Dear Solovine,
The exchange of letters with a South African schoolgirl which you refer to was a dismal failure. The main outcome was astonishment at the news that I had not been dead for 300 years (confusion with Newton).
I am here in Florida for three weeks, with four more days to go. The operation was a stomach incision based on a conjecture which was not entirely correct. I have made a good recovery and the operation was not useless, because certain defects were corrected. But I am still weakened, for at this age one can no longer expect very much.
With cordial regards to you and your wife,

Your

A. Einstein

Lieber Solovine!

Ich bin ganz gerührt über Ihren herzlichen Brief, der so sehr absticht von den andern unzähligen Briefen, die bei dieser mißlichen Gelegenheit auf mich niedergeprasselt sind. Sie stellen es so vor, dass ich mit stiller Befriedigung auf ein Lebenswerk zurücksehen. Aber es ist ganz anders von der Nähe gesehen. Da ist kein einziger Begriff, von dem ich überzeugt wäre, dass er standhalten werd, und ich fühle mich unsicher, ob ich überhaupt auf dem rechten Wege bin. Die Zeitgenossen aber sehen in mir zugleich einen Ketzer und Reaktionär, der sich selber sozusagen überlebt hat. Das hat allerdings mit Mode und Kurzsichtigkeit zu schaffen, aber das Gefühl der Unzulänglichkeit kommt von innen. Nun – es kann wohl nicht anders sein, wenn man kritisch und ehrlich ist, und Humor und Bescheidung halten einen im Gleichgewicht, der äußeren Erwartungen zum Trotz.

Sie haben weiss Gott recht mit dem, was Sie über die Erfahrungen mit den Menschen sagen. Aber keiner kann ja anders, als er eben thut. Das Schmerzlichste ist das Soziale, das sich im grossen Rahmen abspielt. Dies Dominieren des blind Triebhaften. Amerika, England Russland und die Kleineren – hol sie der Teufel, und er wird es auch thun.

Das Beste, was bleibt, sind ein paar aufrechte Freunde, die Kopf und Herz am rechten Fleck haben und einander verstehen, so wie es bei uns beiden ist.

Ich bin neugierig, was Sie über den Heraklit zusammengebracht haben. Ich denke mir, dass er ein trotziger und finsterer Geselle gewesen ist. Es ist zu schade, dass diese Riesenkerle nur durch einen dicken Nebel gesehen werden können.

Alles Herzliche, auch Ihrer Frau

March 28, 1949

Dear Solovine,

I was deeply moved by your affectionate letter, which contrasts so sharply with the countless other letters that have reached me on this unhappy occasion. You imagine that I regard my life's work with calm satisfaction. But a close look yields a completely different picture. I am not convinced of the certainty of a simple concept, and I am uncertain as to whether I was even on the right track. In me my contemporaries see both a heretic and reactionary who has, so to speak, survived himself. That, to be sure, is a matter of fashion and short-sightedness, but the feeling of inadequacy comes from within. Well, it can not be otherwise when one has a critical mind and is honest, and mood and modesty keep us in balance in spite of external influences.

God knows how right you are in everything you say about human experience. But whatever is done justly cannot be done otherwise. What is most grievous is the social drama which is being played on the world stage. This domination of blind impulses. America, England, Russia and the smaller ones—may the devil take them, and he will.

The best that remains are some upright friends whose heads and hearts are in the right place and who understand each other, as we two do.

I am curious about the material you have assembled on Heraclitus. I think that he was a stubborn, melancholy man. It is a pity that these gigantic individuals can be seen only through a thick fog.

My very best, to you and your wife.

Yours,

A. Einstein

25. I 50.

Lieber Solovine!

Ich habe Ihnen einen dicken Band zugesandt, weil einiges darin Sie vermutlich interessieren wird, auch meine kleinen Kontroversen mit den Fachkollegen. Bald werde ich Ihnen auch die neue Auflage meines Büchleins übersenden mit dem Anhang, der vor ein paar Wochen in den Blättern ein starkes Rauschen erzeugt hat, obwohl niemand ausser dem Übersetzer das Ding zu Gesicht bekommen hat. Es ist wahrhaft drollig: Lorbeeren auf Vorschuss! – Ausserdem sende ich Ihnen in ein paar Wochen ein Büchlein mit gelegentlich entstandenen Aufsätzen etc., sobald sie gedruckt sind. Der sonderbare Briefwechsel mit (ungebildeten) russischen Akademikern ist dabei.

Ich hoffe, dass das Leben in Paris auch für Nicht-profiteurs allmählich erträglicher wird, und dass es Dir und Deiner Frau gut geht. Bei uns ist es auch befriedigend, was das Privatleben anlangt. Herzliche Grüsse von Ihrem

A. Einstein.

January 25, 1950

Dear Solovine,

I sent you a thick volume thinking that certain things in it would probably interest you, among them my little quarrels with professional physicists. Soon I shall also send you the new edition of my book with the Appendix which produced so much excitement in the newspapers a few weeks ago even though no one, except the translator, had seen it. This is really amusing: laurels given out in advance! I shall also send you another book containing essays composed at odd intervals as soon as they are printed. It contains the odd exchange of letters between me and the (so-called) Russian academicians.

I hope that life in Paris is gradually becoming tolerable for the non-black marketeers, and that you are well, you and your wife. Our own private life is satisfactory.

Cordial greetings from
Your

A. Einstein

den 12. Juni 1950

Lieber Solovine,

Anbei erhalten Sie die Bestätigung die an Gauthiers-Villars gegangen ist. Es wäre richtiger, wenn der Anhang gleich in der Form erschiene, die er in der gegenwärtig in Vorbereitung befindlichen vierten Auflage der Vorlesungen enthält. Die verallgemeinerte Gravitationstheorie ist darin von einem Ueberlegungsfehler befreit und auch sonst verbessert.

Mit dem von Ihnen vorgeschlagenen Titel für "Out of my later Years" bin ich einverstanden. Wenn Sie noch kein Exemplar dieses Buches von mir erhalten haben, schreiben Sie es mir bitte; ich werde Ihnen dann eines senden.

Mit der Frage der Statistik versus Determinismus ist es so: Vom Standpunkt der unmittelbaren Erfahrung gibt es keinen exacten Determinismus. In dieser Beziehung besteht volle Uebereinstimmung. Die Frage ist, ob die theoretische Beschreibung der Natur deterministisch sein soll oder nicht. Darüber hinaus besteht insbesondere die Frage, ob es überhaupt ein begriffliches Bild der Wirklichkeit (für den Einzelfall) gibt, das im Prinzip vollständig und frei ist von Statistik. Darüber allein bestehen Meinungsdifferenzen.

Herzliche Grüsse
Ihr
A. Einstein.

June 12, 1950

Dear Solovine,

Enclosed herewith is the confirmation sent to Gauthier-Villars. It would be more appropriate to have the Appendix appear in the same format as in the fourth edition of the Lectures, now in preparation. The theory of gravitation has had one mistake in logic deleted and has been corrected.

I agree with you about the title which you propose to substitute for *Out of My Later Years*. If you have not yet received from me a copy of my book, write to me, please, and I will send you one.

Concerning the question of Statistics against Determinism, this is the way it appears: From the point of view of immediate experience there is no such thing as exact determinism. Here there is no disagreement. The question is whether or not the theoretical description of nature must be deterministic. Beyond that, the question is whether or not there exists generally a conceptual image of reality (for the isolated case), an image which is in principle completely exempt from statistics. Only on this subject do opinions differ.

With cordial regards
Your

A. Einstein

den 10. Juli 1950

Lieber Solovine,

Ich erhielt Ihren Brief vom 30. Juni und bin mit
all Ihren Vorschlägen einverstanden. Die Sache mit den
Spektrallinien ist natürlich darauf zurückzuführen, dass
ich mich um die Herausgabe der Aufsätze nicht gekümmert
habe und dass die Herausgeber keine Ahnung von der Sache
haben. Neugierig bin ich, inwiefern wir über die Religion
verschiedener Meinung sein können. Ich kann mir nicht vor-
stellen, dass unsere Meinungen irgendwie wesentlich von
einander abweichen. Wenn es so scheint habe ich mich
wahrscheinlich schlecht ausgedrückt.

Mir persönnlich geht es recht befriedigend, aber
meine Schwester ist sehr zurückgegangen, immerhin ohne
sonderlich darunter zu leiden.

Die nächste Auflage des Anhanges ist immer noch dadurch verzögert, dass ich keinen völlig befriedigenden Be-
weis für die Kompatibilität der neuen Feldgleichungen gefunden habe. Daher die Verzögerung.

Mit herzlichen Grüssen
Ihr
A. E.

July 10, 1950

Dear Solovine,

I received your letter of June 30 and agree to all your proposals. The matter of spectral rays is of course explained by the fact that I had nothing at all do with the publication of my essays and the publishers had no notion of the subject. I am curious to learn just how far our opinions on religion differ. I can not imagine how, basically, our opinions could be widely divergent. If that is the way it appears, I probably failed to express myself clearly.

Personally I am getting along well, though my sister has retrogressed, without suffering much, however.

The next edition of the Appendix is still being held up because I can find no completely satisfactory proof for the compatibility of the new field equations. Hence the delay.

With my cordial greetings,
Yours

A. E.

den 1. Januar 1951

Lieber Solovine:

Vielen Dank für Ihren ausführlichen Brief vom 7 Dezember. Zu Ihren Fragen :

Die Militarisierung Deutschlands hat doch schon kurz nach 1848 eingesetzt, seit Preussen Einfluss gewann, wo die Militarisierung viel älteren Datums ist. Ich glaube, dass hundert Jahre die beste kurze Bezeichnung der Zeitdauer für den Prozess ist.-

Schluss des Aufsatzes über Kepler: Die Bemerkung soll den Leser auf diesen psychologischen und historischen interessanten Punkt aufmerksam machen. Kepler hat zwar die damals übliche Astrologie abgelehnt, aber doch dem Gedanken Ausdruck gegeben, dass die Möglichkeit einer vernünftigen Astrologie durchaus bestehe. Dies ist gar nicht so merkwürdig, weil die Vermutung animistischer kausaler Zusammenhänge, wie sie dem Primitiven fast überall eigentümlich ist, nicht an sich unvernünftig ist, und von der Naturwissenschaft unter dem Druck der systematisch gewonnenen Erfahrungen nur allmählich verlassen wurde. Keplers Forschungen haben natürlich sehr zu diesem Prozess beigetragen, der sich in seinem eigenen Geist als ein harter innerer Kampf abgespielt hat.

Ihre Abneigung gegen den Gebrauch des Wortes "Religion", wenn es sich um eine emotionale seelische Einstellung handelt, die in Spinoza am deutlichsten hervortritt, kann ich sehr wohl begreifen. Ich habe keinen besseren Ausdruck als den Ausdruck "religiös" für dieses Vertrauen in die vernünftige und der der menschlichen Vernunft wenigstens einigermassen zugängliche Beschaffenheit der Realität. Wo dieses Gefühl fehlt, da artet Wissenschaft in geistlose Empirie aus. Es schert mich einen Teufel, wenn die Pfaffen daraus Kapital schlagen. Dagegen ist ohnehin kein Kraut gewachsen.

January 1, 1951

Dear Solovine,

Many thanks for your detailed letter of December 7. Here are the answers to your questions:

The militarization of Germany came about shortly after 1848 following the rise of Prussia, where militarization had a much earlier beginning. I believe that one century is the best rough designation of the length of the process.

Conclusion of the article on Kepler: The remark will draw attention to this psychological and historically interesting point. Kepler did reject the astrology of his era but still promoted the idea that the existence of rational astrology is entirely possible. This is not so extraordinary, for the positing of causal animistic connections, which is almost always characteristic of primitive man, is not unreasonable in itself, and was given up only gradually by science under the pressure of systematically acquired data. Kepler's research doubtless contributed much to the process, which developed as a harsh inner struggle in his mind.

I can well understand your aversion to the use of the word "religion" when what is meant is an emotional or psychological attitude, which is most obvious in Spinoza. I have found no better expression than "religious" for confidence in the rational nature of reality insofar as it is accessible to human reason. Wherever this feeling is absent, science degenerates into uninspired empiricism. For all I care, the parsons can make capital of it. Anyway, nothing can be done about it.

Ihrer Kritik bezüglich Wissenschaft und Moral, bezw.
Zielsetzung, kann ich mich nicht anschliessen. Was wir
Wissenschaft nennen hat ausschliesslich das Ziel, festzu-
stellen was ist. Die Bestimmung darüber was sein soll ist
etwas davon Unabhängiges, nicht auf methodischem Wege
Erreichbares. Die Wissenschaft kann nur Sätze über Moral in
logischen Susammenhang bringen und Mittel zur Verwirklichung
moralischer Ziele liefern, aber die Zielsetzung selbst ist
ausserhalb ihrer Domäne. Das ist wenigstens meine Ansicht.
Wenn Sie aber nicht mit mir übereinstimmen, dann frage ich
gehorsamst: wessen Blödsinn soll in diesem Buche Platz finden, meiner oder Ihrer?

Mit herzlichen Grüssen und Wünschen für 1951

Ihr

A. Einstein

I can not concur in you opinion concerning science and ethics or the determination of aims. What we call science has the sole purpose of determining what *is*. The determining of what *ought to be* is unrelated to it and can not be accomplished methodically. Science can only arrange ethical propositions logically and furnish the means for the realization of ethical aims, but the determination of aims is beyond its scope. At least that is the way I see it. But if you do not agree with me, I respectfully ask, which imbecility should find a place in the book, yours or mine?

With cordial greetings and best wishes for 1951.

Your

A. Einstein

den 12. Februar 1951

Lieber Solovine:

Im deutschen Text habe ich damals "begrenzt" geschrieben in dem Sinne von "zu wenig allgemein verbreitet".

Mit den beiden Verlegern ist es fatal, weil Flammarion einen Vertrag hat, den ich aus Nachlässigkeit habe durchschlüpfen lassen (mein Freund und Mitarbeiter Infeld hat es damals besorgt), von dem es zweifelhaft ist, inwieweit es der Firma Flammarion Rechte auf dieses Buch gibt. Ich hoffe sehr, dass Sie die mühevolle Uebersetzung bezahlt bekommen haben. Wenn dies der Fall ist, dann liegt mir eigentlich nicht viel daran, dass das Buch erscheint.- Die Verlage mögen es untereinander ausmachen.

Das Leiden meiner Schwester ist natürlich in der Zwischenzeit weiter vorgeschritten, ohne dass sie direkt darunter zu leiden hätte. Ich selber bin mit meinem Zustand zufrieden, wenn sich auch das Alter natürlich bemerkbar macht. Ich bin nämlich nicht aus einer langlebigen Familie.

Die einheitliche Feldtheorie ist nun in sich abgeschlossen. Sie ist aber so schwer mathematisch anzuwenden, dass ich trotz aller aufgewendeten Mühe nicht imstande bin, sie irgendwie zu prüfen. Dieser Zustand wird wohl noch viele Jahre anhalten, zumal die Physiker für logisch-philosophische Argumente wenig Verständnis haben.

Mit herzlichen Grüssen
Ihr
A. Einstein -

February 12, 1951

Dear Solovine,

In the German text I wrote "limited" in the sense of "not too common."

The editorial mix-up is unfortunate, for Flammarion is in possession of a contract which I negligently let slip through (my friend and collaborator Infeld is looking into it now); the extent to which Flammarion is entitled to publication rights is still in doubt. I hope that you have been paid for the translation, which was marked by so many difficulties. If so, publication matters little to me, to be truthful. Let the publishers arrange matters between themselves.

My sister's affliction has naturally become increasingly severe in the interval, but she does not suffer from it directly. I myself can not complain of my health, although the effects of old age are making themselves felt. I do not come from a long-lived family, as you know.

The unified field theory has been brought to a conclusion. But it is hard to use it mathematically for, in spite of all the trouble I have gone to, I am not able to verify it in any way. This state of affairs will last for many more years, mainly because physicists have no understanding of logical and philosophical arguments.

Cordial regards,
Your

A. Einstein

den 23. März 1951

Lieber Solovine:

Ich danke Ihnen herzlich für Ihren lieben Brief und für das Büchlein von la Mettrie mit Ihrem interessanten Vorwort. Es wird einem nicht leicht zu realisieren, dass die Gebildeten des 18. Jahrhunderts das Büchlein revolutionär gefunden haben. Ich lese meiner Schwester jeden Abend ein Stück daraus vor. Sie würden lachen, wenn Sie meine gestammelten französischen Tönchen hören könnten. Was einem bei der Lektüre auch wundert ist der blumige Rokoko-Stil, der von dem nüchternen Geist unserer Zeit so grell absticht.

Ich denke mir manchmal, wie wohl der Solo die internationalen politischen Pfuschereien beurteilt. Wahrscheinlich sind wir sehr verschiedener Ansicht, weil jeder geneigt ist, gegen das was in seiner Nähe ist, am sauersten zu reagieren.

Bei uns geht es soweit gut, aber mit meiner Schwester ist es unterdessen weiter abwärts gegangen. Sie kann kaum mehr ein verständliches Wort herausbringen, obwohl sie noch ganz gut denken kann.

Herzlich grüsst Sie
Ihr
A. Einstein.

March 23, 1951

Dear Solovine,

I thank you sincerely for your amiable letter and for the book by La Mettrie with your interesting Foreword. It is not easy to understand how cultured people of the 18th century found this book revolutionary. I read a part of it to my sister every evening. You would laugh if you could hear me stammer out the precious French sounds. The reader is also struck by the flowery rococo style, which contrasts so sharply with the heavy spirit of our time.

I sometimes wonder how Solo looks upon international political blunderings. Our outlook is probably different, for each is inclined to react most bitterly against what is close at hand.

All is well with us, but my sister's condition has worsened in the inverval. She can scarcely pronounce an intelligible word, though her mind is still clear.

Cordial regards to you
Your

A. Einstein

den 29. März 1951

Lieber Solovine:

Ich sende Ihnen hiermit die Correctur zurück. Ich habe meine Bemerkungen deutsch geschrieben; wenn Sie es nicht verstehen, dann fragen Sie mich wieder. Ich merke übrigens, dass auch nach Berichtigungen der Appendix über Verallgemeinerte Gravitationstheorie ziemlich schwer zu verstehen ist. Es ist wichtiger, dass die Sache verständlich sei als dass sie möglichst früh erscheint.

Die Sache mit den Packeten tut mir sehr leid. Schiller "Ring des Polykrates" kam mir in den Sinn. Erkundigen Sie sich doch, ob die sogenannten "Care"-Packete ebenfalls mit hohem Zoll belegt sind. Diesen ganzen Segen habt Ihr dem Truman und seinen Helfern zu verdanken.

Wegen des Buches brauchen Sie sich keinen Kummer zu machen, nachdem Sie die Uebersetzung bezahlt bekommen haben. Ich habe keine Illusion, mit diesem Buche die Welt verbessern zu können und es ist mir wurst, wenn es erst später oder überhaupt nicht erscheint. Jedenfalls werde ich mich nicht hineinmischen. Sollte es doch zur Publikation kommen, können wir uns immer noch wegen des Bildes den Kopf zerbrechen.

Die Sache wegen der Schrödinger Gleichung ist ganz in Ordnung. ε ist eine Funktion von q und p allein. Die aus dem ε fabrizierte Schrödinger Funktion psi hängt aber von der Zeit t ab.

Der La Mettrie ist interessant geschrieben, wenn auch die vielen Rokokoblumen uns dabei kurios anmuten. Ich habe alles meiner Schwester vorgelesen. Schwer zu denken, dass die Zeitgenossen das als so aufreizend empfunden haben.

Mit herzlichen Grüssen von uns allen
Ihr
A. Einstein.

March 29, 1951

Dear Solovine,

I am sending the correction herewith. I wrote my comments in German; if you do not understand them, write me again. I notice besides that even after the corrections the Appendix on the theory of gravitation is quite difficult to understand. It is more important for the subject to be intelligible than for the volume to appear as soon as possible.

I am very sorry about the package mix-up. Schiller's "The Ring of Polycrates" comes to mind. Find out whether the so-called "Care" packages are subject to high duties too. You owe this whole blessing to Truman and his helpers.

There is no need for you to bother about the book after having been paid for the translation. I have no illusion of being able to better the world through this book, and it makes no difference to me whether the book appears later or not at all. In any case, I do not intend to be mixed up in it. If it is published, we can always bash our heads in over the portrait.

Schrödinger's equation is wholly in order. E is a function of q and p alone. But Schrödinger's function psi, formed from E, depends on the time t.

La Mettrie writes interestingly, though we were struck by his flowery rococo style. I read all of it to my sister. It is hard to understand how his contemporaries managed to find it so exciting.

With warmest greetings from all of us.

Your

A. Einstein

den 30. Juli 1951

Lieber Solovine:

Ich erhielt Ihre liebe Karte vom 16. Juli. Die zwei un-
schuldigen Druckfehler nehmen sich gegenüber den sonstigen
Teufeleien der Menschen recht bescheiden aus.

Ich habe Ihnen die traurige Mitteilung zu machen, dass
meine liebe Schwester schon vor vier Wochen durch einen sanften
Tod von ihrem grässlichen Leiden erlöst wurde. Eine plötzliche
Verschlimmerung der Hirn-Arteriosklerose hatte einen leichten
Fall zur Folge, der aber einen komplizierten Bruch des rechten
Oberarms verursachte. Das hierdurch notwendig gewordene Still-
liegen führte zu einer Lungenentzündung mit hohem Fieber und
Bewusstlosigkeit, die den Tod nach etwa 10 Tagen herbeiführte.
Bis zu diesem Unfall habe ich ihr allabendlich vorgelesen, zu-
mal ihre geistige Kraft - abgesehen vom Gedächtnis für neue
Eindrücke - kaum gelitten hatte. Ich bin sicher, Sie werden
der guten Seele ein freundliches Andenken wahren.

Man plagt sich redlich, aber der prekäre Gott Spinozas
hat es uns noch weit schwieriger gemacht als unsere Väter
ahnten.

Mit herzlichen Grüssen
Ihr
A. Einstein

July 30, 1951

Dear Solovine,

I received your delightful card of July 16. The two innocent printing mistakes are insignificant in contrast with the diabolical machinations of men.

I must transmit to you the sad news that my dear sister was delivered from her horrible suffering by a gentle death four weeks ago. An acute aggravation of the arteriosclerosis of the brain was responsible for a slight fall resulting in a compound fracture of the right arm. This necessitated complete rest, which brought about an attack of pneumonia accompanied by a high fever and loss of consciousness. Death came in about ten days. Up until the accident, I used to read to her every evening, so long as her intellectual stamina—with the exception of remembrance of new impressions—was relatively unimpaired. I am sure that you will remember the good soul kindly.

We bear many afflictions unflinchingly, but Spinoza's precarious God has made our task more difficult than our forefathers suspected.

With cordial regards,
Your

A. Einstein

30.III.52.

Lieber Solovine!

Ich habe mich wie stets auch mit Ihrem letzten Briefe sehr gefreut. Mit den von Ihnen vorgeschlagenen Änderungen bin ich durchaus einverstanden.

Was nun den Carl Seelig anlangt, so ist er ein braver Mensch. Er nimmt es aber leider nur zu ernst mit der von ihm übernommenen Aufgabe, sodass er alle Welt damit molestiert. Sagen Sie ihm, was Sie für gut halten und verschweigen Sie auch, was Sie wollen. Denn es ist doch nicht gut, wenn man sozusagen nackt einer sogar sehr neutralen – Öffentlichkeit präsentiert wird. Treffen Sie Ihre Entscheidungen selber und machen Sie mir keine Mitteilung davon. Denn ich will mich auch nicht indirekt in diese Unternehmung einmischen. Ich habe ihm allerdings einige sachliche Anfragen beantwortet.

Nun komme ich zu dem interessantesten Punkt Ihres Briefes. Sie finden es merkwürdig, dass ich die Begreiflichkeit der Welt (soweit wir berechtigt sind, von einer solchen zu sprechen) als Wunder oder ewiges Geheimnis empfinde. Nun, a priori sollte man doch eine chaotische Welt erwarten, die durch Denken in keiner Weise fassbar ist. Man könnte (ja sollte) erwarten, dass die Welt nur insoweit als gesetzlich erweise, als wir ordnend eingreifen. Es wäre eine Art Ordnung wie die alphabetische Ordnung der Worte einer Sprache. Die Art Ordnung, die dagegen z. B. durch Newtons Gravitations-Theorie geschaffen wird, ist von ganz anderem Charakter. Wenn auch die Axiome der Theorie vom Menschen gesetzt sind, so setzt doch der Erfolg eines solchen Beginnens eine hochgradige Ordnung der objektiven Welt voraus, die a priori zu erwarten man keinerlei Berechtigung hatte. Hier liegt das „Wunder", das sich mit der Entwicklung unserer Kenntnisse nur immer mehr verstärkt.

Hier liegt der schwache Punkt für die Positivisten und die berufsmässigen Atheisten, die sich beglückt fühlen durch das Bewusstsein, die Welt erfolgreich nicht nur entgöttert sondern sogar „entwundert" zu haben. Das Schöne ist, dass wir uns mit der Anerkennung des „Wunders" bescheiden müssen, ohne dass es einen legitimen Weg darüber hinaus gibt. Dies muss ich ausdrücklich hinzufügen, damit Sie nicht denken, ich sei – geschwächt durch das Alter – eine Beute der Pfaffen geworden. –

Nach Europa gehe ich nicht mehr, um nicht unnötigerweise der Mittelpunkt einer Affenkomödie zu werden. Alles ist ja für jeden heutzutage ohnehin so unheimlich nahe, dass man weniger als je danach reisen muss.

March 30, 1952

Dear Solovoine,

As always, I was delighted by your last letter. As for the changes proposed by you, I am in complete agreement.

Carl Seelig is a good man. But he takes the task that he has undertaken far too seriously, alas, with the result that he bothers everyone. Tell him whatever you think best and pass over whatever you wish in silence. For it is not always good to be presented to the public nude—or rather neuter. Make your decisions but do not communicate them to me, for I do not wish to be mixed up, even indirectly, in this affair. I did of course answer a few positive requests.

Now I come to the most interesting point in your letter. You find it strange that I consider the comprehensibility of the world (to the extent that we are authorized to speak of such a comprehensibility) as a miracle or as an eternal mystery. Well, *a priori* one should expect a chaotic world which cannot be grasped by the mind in any way. One could (yes *one should*) expect the world to be subjected to law only to the extent that we order it through our intelligence. Ordering of this kind would be like the alphabetical ordering of the words of a language. By contrast, the kind of order created by Newton's theory of gravitation, for instance, is wholly different. Even if the axioms of the theory are proposed by man, the success of such a project presupposes a high degree of ordering of the objective world, and this could not be expected *a priori*. That is the "miracle" which is being constantly reinforced as our knowledge expands.

Uns geht es hier allen nach Wunsch, auch Margot, die durch die Operation viel widerstandsfähiger geworden ist. Ich habe in der Ableitung der nicht symmetrischen Feldtheorie eine wichtige Ergänzung gefunden, welche die allgemeinen Feldgleichungen ebenso a priori bestimmt wie das nackte Relativitätsprinzip die Gravitationsgleichungen.

Mit herzlichen Grüssen an Sie beide Ihr

A. E.

There lies the weakness of positivists and professional atheists who are elated because they feel that they have not only successfully rid the world of gods but "bared the miracles." Oddly enough, we must be satisfied to acknowledge the "miracle" without there being any legitimate way for us to approach it. I am forced to add that just to keep you from thinking that—weakened by age—I have fallen pray to the parsons.

All of us here are well, including Margot who, thanks to her operation, has developed more resistance. In the elaboration of the nonsymmetrical field theory I have found an important complement which determines the general equations of the field *a priori* just as the simple principle of relativity determined the equations of gravitation.

With warmest regards to you both.

Your

A. E.

I do not intend to go to Europe again in order to avoid being the central figure in a monkey farce. Besides, everything today is so close to each of us that there is less justification than ever for chasing after it.

7. V. 52

Lieber Solo!

In Ihrem Brief geben Sie mir für zwei Stunden auf
den Popo. Die erste Sünde ist unkritisches Verhalten inbezug
auf den Plan für world government. Immerhin behandeln Sie
es nicht als unerwünscht sondern als in absehbarer Zeit nicht
erreichbar. Sie geben gute Gründe für die Nicht-Erreichbarkeit.
Sie hätten noch dazu mit gutem Gründen die Furcht äussern
können, dass die Weltregierung unerträglicher und insbesondere
ungerechter sein könnte als der jetzige Zustand der Anarchie.
Man denke an die Segnungen der U. N. für die Leute in Korea!
Auf der anderen Seite aber steht die Gefahr der völligen Selbst-
vernichtung der Menschheit, eine Sache, die für uns doch
einen Gewicht haben sollte. Deshalb sollten wir mindestens der "unerwünschten" (wenn auch zögernd) zustreben.

Mit dem "unmöglich" ist es so eine Sache. Es verwandelt
sich nämlich in ein "möglich", wenn die Menschen es
ernsthaft wollen, wenn auch nur aus Furcht der einen
Zustand unerträglicher Unsicherheit. Solchen Zustand des Wollens
herbeizuführen, sollte man mit allen Kräften versuchen.
Diese Bemühung ist nützlich, selbst in dem Falle, dass das
Ziel nicht erreicht wird, denn sie hat gewiss eine günstige
erzieherische Wirkung, indem sie sich gegen den dummen und
verlogenen vollen Nationalismus wendet.

May 7, 1952

Dear Solovine,

In your letter you blame me for having committed two sins. First, for having taken an uncritical attitude regarding the plan for a world government. You always look upon it, not as undesirable, but as something that cannot be realized in the near future. You give good reasons to prove that it can not be realized. You might have added as still another good reason the fear that the world government would be more unbearable and especially more unjust that the present state of anarchy. Just think of the benefits brought to Korea by the United Nations! But on the other hand, humanity faces the danger of self-annihilation, something which should weigh down on us. For that reason we should withdraw (though hesitantly) the "undesirable."

As for the "impossible," this much can be said: it becomes "possible" if men *seriously will* it, even if this is brought about solely by their fear of living in an unbearable state of insecurity. We must exert every effort to create this desire. The effort will be worthwhile even if the aim is not achieved, for it will certainly have some educational merit in that it will be directed against stupid, heinous nationalism.

[Handwritten German text]

Nun sagen Sie dass man zuerst die Jugend zur objektiven Betrachtung der historischen Dinge erziehen solle. Dann erst würde sich auf dem politischen Felde etwas erhoffen dürfen. Mit dieser Priorität ist es aber wie mit der von Ei und Henne. D. h. wir stehen vor einem circulus vitiosus. Die Henne ist die politische Ordnung und das Ei die vernünftige Erziehung. Wenn es nun auch kein Ende dieses Knäuels gibt, sondern aus er sich entwirren liesse, so muss man es eben überall probieren und dabei den Mut nicht verlieren.

Wenn aber alle Bemühung nichts hilft, und die Menschen in Selbst-Zerstörung enden, so wird ihnen der Kosmos keine Thräne nachweinen. Nur gut, dass wenigstens das Buch noch vorher auf dem Markte erschienen ist — ausgedruckt. Ich sehe die Sache schematisch so

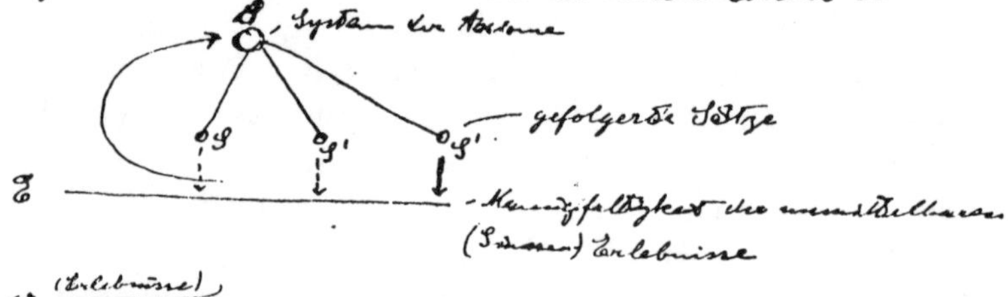

[Handwritten diagram with labels: "System der Axiome", "gefolgerte Sätze", "Mannigfaltigkeit der unmittelbaren (Sinnen-) Erlebnisse", points labeled A, S, S', S'', and E]

(1) Die E (Erlebnisse) sind uns gegeben.

(2) A sind die Axiome, aus denen wir Folgerungen ziehen. Psychologisch beruhen die A auf E. Es gibt aber keinen logischen Weg von der E zu A, sondern nur einen intuitiven (psychologischen) Zusammenhang, der immer „auf Widerruf" ist.

(3) Aus A werden auf logischem Wege Einzel-Aussagen S abgeleitet, welche Ableitungen den Anspruch auf Richtigkeit erheben können.

You say that we should start by training the young people to examine historical events objectively. Only in this way could we hope to realize anything in politics. But this is a chicken-and-egg relationship or a vicious circle. The chicken is the political situation and the egg is rational training. Since the skein offers no loose end to enable us to unravel it, we simply have to make every possible attempt and not lose our courage.

But if every effort fails and men end by destroying themselves, the universe will not shed a single tear for them. It would still be good, however, if the book could at least appear first and be placed on sale.

As for the epistemological question, you completely misunderstood me; I probably expressed myself badly. I see the matter schematically in this way:

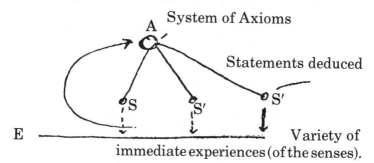

(1) The E's (immediate experiences) are our data.
(2) The axioms from which we draw our conclusions are indicated by A. Psychologically the A's depend on the E's. But there is no logical route leading from the E's to the A's, but only an intuitive connection (psychological), which is always "re-turning."
(3) *Logically*, specific statements S, S', S'' are deduced from A; these statements can lay claim to exactness.

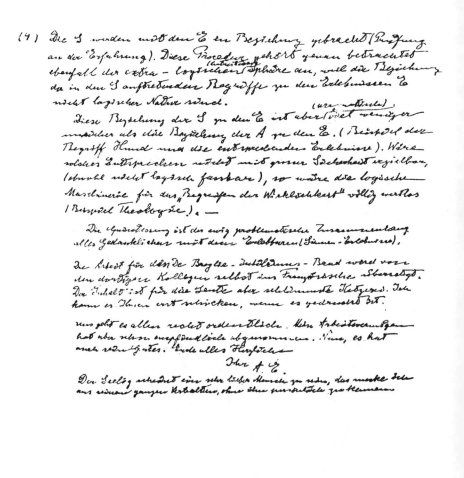

(4)   The A's are connected to the E's (verification through experience). Closer examination shows that this procedure also belongs to the extralogical (intuitive) sphere, for the relation between the notions show up in S and the immediate experiences are not logical in nature.

But the relation between S's and E's is (pragmatically) much less certain than the relation between the A's and the E's. (Take the notion "dog" and the corresponding immediate experiences.) If such a relationship could not be set up with a high degree of certainty (though it may be beyond the reach of logic), logical machinery would have no value in the "comprehension of reality" (example: theology).

What this all boils down to is the eternally problematical connection between the world of ideas and that which can be experienced (immediate experiences of the senses).

The work for the de Broglie anniversary volume will be translated into French by scholars there. But its contents will be a heresy of the worst order for the people. I can not send it to you until it is printed.

We are all well, but my capacity for work has lessened perceptibly; even that has its good side.

Warmest regards to you.

Your

A. E.

Seelig is a likeable man, to judge by his behavior and without knowing him personally.

den 17. November 1952

Lieber Solovine:

Ich habe die englische Uebersetzung dieser kleinen Aufsätze, die in dem Buch gesammelt sind, lange nicht so ernst genommen, wie Sie bei Ihrer Uebersetzung. Ihr englischer Ausdruck für die Leiter der Elektrizität ist wahrscheinlich besser als der auf Seite 234 gegebene. Das Wort "report" auf Seite 111 meint "mitteilen". Es mag sein, dass der englische Ausdruck nicht adequat ist, ich denke aber, man versteht was gemeint ist.

Dem Dr. Lowe geht es ganz gut. Er ist gegenwärtig in Europa (Schweiz) und wird Sie sicher besuchen wenn er nach Paris kommt.

Sie dürfen sich nicht beklagen über die Torheiten und Irrungen Ihrer Landsleute. Es wäre doch zu anmassend, wenn sie allen Anderen gegenüber eine Ausnahme bilden würden. Die Meinigen philosophieren schon kräftig darüber, warum sie in Europa nicht so sonderlich beliebt sind. Alles wäre doch so possierlich, wenn man nicht selber dem Gesindel mit Haut und Haaren ausgeliefert wäre.

Was mich betrifft, habe ich eine Venenentzündung hinter mir, die sonst hauptsächlich bei schwangeren Frauen aufzutreten pflegt. Jetzt aber geht es uns Allen bis auf weiteres befriedigend.

Unsere Akademische "Olympia" ist durch den guten Seelig verherrlicht und der Unsterblichkeit zugeführt worden, wie sie es verdient. Unsere übermütigen Abende aber hat der Meister doch nicht wieder zum Leben erwecken können - leider.

Einstweilen herzliche Grüsse für Sie und Ihre Frau

Ihr

A. Einstein.

November 17, 1952

Dear Solovine,

I did not take the translation of the book of collected essays half so seriously as you. Your English expression for conductors of electricity is probably better than the one used on page 234. The word "report" on p. 111 means "communicate." It is possible that the English expression is not adequate, but I think that its meaning will be understood.

Dr. Lowe is fine. He is now in Europe (Switzerland) and will certainly visit you when he is in Paris.

You must not complain about the imbecilities and mistakes of your compatriots. It would be too much to expect them to be an exception to all the others. Mine are getting a workout in philosophy by asking themselves why they are not especially loved in Europe. Everything would really be comical if we were not altogether at the mercy of the rabble.

I myself have just gotten rid of phlebitis, which normally shows up in pregnant women. Now we are all, until something new develops, in good health.

Our academic "Olympia" was glorified and escorted to immortality by good old Seelig, as it deserved to be. But the master could not bring our high-spirited evenings back to life—alas!

In the meantime warmest greetings to you and your wife.

Your

A. Einstein

An die unsterbliche Akademie Olympia.

In deinem kurzen aktiven Dasein hast du in kindlicher Freude dich ergötzt an allem was klar und gescheit war. Deine Mitglieder haben dich geschaffen, um sich über deine grossen, alten und aufgeblasenen Schwestern lustig zu machen. Wie sehr sie damit das Richtige getroffen haben, hab ich durch langjährige sorgfältige Beobachtungen voll zu würdigen gelernt.

Wir alle drei Mitglieder haben uns zum Mindesten als dauerhaft erwiesen. Wenn sie auch schon etwas kränkelig sind, so strahlt doch noch etwas von deinem heitern und belebenden Licht auf unsern einsamen Lebenspfad, denn du bist nicht mit ihnen alt geworden und ausgewachsen wie eine ins Kraut gewachsene Salatpflanze.

Dir gilt meine Treue und Anhänglichkeit bis zum letzten hochgelehrten Schnaufer! Das nunmehr nur korrespondierende Mitglied

A. E.

Princeton 3. IV. 53.

To the immortal Olympia academy,

In your short active existence you took a childish delight in all that was clear and reasonable. Your members created you to amuse themselves at the expense of your big sisters who were older and puffed up with pride. I learned fully to appreciate just how far they had hit upon the true through careful observations lasting for many long years.

We three members, all of us at least remained steadfast. Though somewhat decrepit, we still follow the solitary path of our life by your pure and inspiring light; for you did not grow old and shapeless along with your members like a plant that goes to seed.

To you I swear fidelity and devotion until my last learned breath! From one who hereafter will be only a corresponding member,

A.E.

Princeton, April 3, 1953

den 23. April 1953

Lieber Solovine:

Vor allem danke ich Ihnen für die stilvolle Antwort
auf meine akademische Botschaft. Diese Antwort hätte eine
Zierde am Hofe Friedrich II. abgeben können.

Wenn Gauthier-Villars die drei erwähnten Publikationen
in einem Bändchen vereinigt neu herausgeben wollen, so habe
ich dagegen nichts einzuwenden. Betreffend das populäre Büchlein habe ich auch nichts gegen eine Publikation. Ich sende
Ihnen hier mein einziges Exemplar der ursprünglichen deutschen
Ausgabe (um deren gelegentliche Rücksendung ich bitte). Zweitens
sende ich Ihnen per Drucksache die letzterschienene Ausgabe, die
mit einigen Ergänzungen versehen ist und drittens eine Copie
eines Anhangs, den ich für die nächstens erscheinende Neu-
auflage der englischen Ausgabe geschrieben habe, und zwar den
ursprünglichen deutschen Text. Auch diesen bitte ich nach
vollendetem Geschäft zurückzusenden, vorausgesetzt, dass diese
Darlegung überhaupt Ihren Beifall finden.

An den Zeitungskritiken habe ich mich gebührend ergötzt.
Ich war gerührt darüber, dass Sie mir eine derselben eigens ab-
geschrieben haben. In dem einen Artikel ist amüsanterweise dem
Alter statt der Jugend das Gefühl der Vereinsamung als schmerz-
lich hervorgehoben.

Mit herzlichen Grüssen
Ihr
A. Einstein.

April 23, 1953

Dear Solovine,

First let me thank you for your grandiloquent answer to my academic message. Your answer would have done honor to the court of Frederick II.

If Gauthier-Villars wants to put the three publications mentioned into one volume for republication, I have no objection. Nor am I opposed to the publication of the popular book. I am sending you my only copy of the original German edition (which I wish you would return as soon as you can). Second, I am sending you a press copy of the last edition, which contains some additions; and third, a copy of an Appendix which I wrote, in German of course, for the new English edition, which is to appear soon. Please return the German text after you have finished the translation, assuming, naturally, that you like this treatise.

I was duly pleased by the newspaper reports. I was deeply moved by your having taken the trouble to copy one of them for me. In one of the articles the sad feeling of loneliness is attributed, amusingly enough, to old age instead of to youth.

With my cordial greetings
Your

A. Einstein

28.V. 53.

Lieber Solo!

Ich habe lachen müssen, dass wir Ihnen ein so traurig defektes Exemplar meiner alten Büchleins geschickt haben. Ich habe überhaupt kein Exemplar mehr, sodass ich Ihre Verbesserungen nicht voll würdigen konnte. Dass Sie nun die Treppen absägen wollen, auf denen die Kinder von geisterhaftem Fackelleben herumgejagt werden, thut mir leid, weil es ein artiges Bild ist. Die Bemerkung wegen der Stange auf dem Platz kann ich nicht billigen. Es kommt mir dort darauf an, den begrifflich nebelhaften „Raum" auf möglichst direkte und einfache (starre Körper) Weise durch etwas erfahrungsmässig Sinnvolles zu ersetzen. Deshalb soll man auch keine optischen Mittel heranziehen.

Streng genommen kann man ja allerdings das Geometrische nicht zurückführen auf „starre" Körper, die es ja genau genommen nicht gibt — ganz abgesehen von der Thatsache, dass feste Körper weit als mensch ... selber angesehen werden dürfen. Auch die Annahme, dass die zur Messung benutzten Körper als Dinge nicht beeinflussen (... selberen ... gehen kann) ist an sich nicht zu rechtfertigen. Es können eben Begriffe nie aus Erlebbarem logisch einwandfrei abgeleitet werden. Aber für didaktische und wohl auch heuristische Zwecke ist solches Vorgehen unvermeidlich. Moral, wenn man gar nicht gegen die Vernunft sündigt, kommt man überhaupt zu nichts, oder auch, man kann kein Haus und keine Brücke bauen ohne Benutzung eines eigentlich nicht dazu gehörigen Gerüstes.

May 28, 1953

Dear Solo,

I had to laugh on learning that we sent you such a sadly incomplete copy of my old book. I have no copy at all now, so that I could not fully appreciate your corrections. That you propose to saw for me the steps which conscientious teachers make their pupils run up and down is disconcerting, though the picture is amusing. I cannot approve of the remark on the subject of the pole in space. There I want to replace abstract and nebulous "space," *as directly and also as simply as possible* (fixed bodies), with something which has meaning, from the point of view of experience, and that is why one should not use an optical expedient.

Strictly speaking, one cannot reduce geometry to "fixed" bodies which, actually, do not exist—without taking into account the fact that fixed bodies should not be looked upon as being divisible *ad infinitum.* Similarly, the supposition that bodies used as standards do not influence objects (supposition which cannot be given a fixed meaning) is itself unjustified. Concepts can never be derived logically from experience and be above criticism. But for didactic and also heuristic purposes such a procedure is inevitable. Moral: Unless one sins against logic, one generally gets nowhere; or, one cannot build a house or construct a bridge without using a scaffold which is really not one of its basic parts.

Die neue Auflage des Brushes Meaning of Relativity mit der neuen Bearbeitung der Verallgemeinerung der Gravitationstheorie werde ich Ihnen zusenden. Es ist natürlich ein Versuch einer Theorie des Gesamtfeldes; aber ich wollte dem Ding keinen so anspruchsvollen Namen geben. Denn ich weiss ja nicht, ob physikalische Wahrheit darin steckt. Vom Standpunkt einer deduktiveren Theorie ist es aber denkbar vollkommen (Sparsamkeit an unabhängigen Begriffen und Hypothesen). Dass man über das Zutreffen oder Nicht-Zutreffen so gar nichts aussagen kann, liegt daran, dass man keine Methoden hat, um die singularitätsfreien Lösungen eines so komplizierten nicht-linearen Gleichungssystems etwas auszusagen oder gar zu berechnen. Dies ist auch der Grund, warum die Physiker nicht geneigt sind, die Sache ernst zu nehmen. Es ist sogar denkbar, dass man es nie wissen wird. Andererseits haben die Theorien, die sich stufenweise an der Beobachtung angeschlossen haben, zu einer unvergleichlichen Häufung der unabhängigen Annahmen geführt. In seinem letzten populären Buche hat de Broglie die Sachlage recht schön charakterisiert. Ich habe nämlich eine englische Ausgabe zugesandt bekommen; die originale französische ist gewiss noch viel besser.
Herzliche Grüsse Ihr A.E.

I am going to send you the new edition of the book *Meaning of Relativity*, which contains the new revision of the theory of gravitation. It is of course an attempt at a theory of the whole field; but I did not wish to give it such a pretentious title, for I am not yet sure that physical truth is at the bottom of it. But from the point of view of a deductive theory, it may be perfect (economy of independent notions and hypotheses). That no one can make a definite statement about its confirmation or non-confirmation results from the fact that there are no methods of affirming anything with respect to solutions that do not yield to the peculiarities of such a complicated non-linear system of equations. It is even possible that no one will ever know. Theories that have gradually developed around what can be observed, however, have led to an intolerable accumulation of independent suppositions. In his last popular book, de Broglie gave a very good description of the situation. I recently received the English edition; the French edition is certainly even better.

Warmest wishes
Your

A. E.

den 15. August 1953

Lieber Solovine:

Es scheint, dass ich vergessen habe, im Drange der Korrespondenz, Ihren Brief vom 15. Juni zu beantworten. Ihre erste Frage kann ich dahin beantworten, dass in Bezug auf ein beschleunigtes System man nicht die Koordinaten so deuten kann, dass die Koordinaten-Differenzen gleich sind den mit Masstäben und Uhren gemessenen Längen bezw. Zeit-Differenzen. Dies kann man sich leicht an den Fällen klar machen, wo das Koordinatensystem gegenüber einem Inertial-system gleichmässig translations-beschleunigt ist, oder gleichförmig rotiert. Damit hängt es zusammen, dass gemäss der allgemeinen Relativitätstheorie das Gravitationsfeld zugleich ein Ausdruck ist für die metrische Struktur von Raum-Zeit.

Wenn die Riemann-Bedingung "satisfaite" ist, dann müssen auch die Gravitations-Gleichungen "satisfaite" sein. Mit anderen Worten, die Gleichungen des Gravitationsfeldes sind eine Spezialisierung der Riemann-Bedingung.

Das deutsche Manuscript des Aufsatzes können Sie behalten, solange Sie es brauchen. Mit Ihren redaktionellen Vorschlägen bin ich natürlich einverstanden.

Es scheint mir, dass Sie nicht nur mein treuer Ueber-setzer, sondern auch mein einziger, wirklich aufmerksamer Leser sind

Mit herzlichen Grüssen

Ihr

A. Einstein

P.S. Ich freue mich über das französische Volk, das nicht ver-gessen hat, seinen Grosskopfeten zu zeigen, wo Gott hockt. (Streik).

August 15, 1953

Dear Solovine,

It seems that, under pressure of correspondence, I forgot to answer your letter of June 15. I can answer your first question by saying that, with respect to an accelerated system, the coordinates can not be interpreted in such a way as to make the differences in the coordinates equal the differences in length corresponding to differences in time as measured by rulers and clocks. This becomes clear in the cases where the system of coordinates is uniformly accelerated with respect a system of inertia, or rotates uniformly. That is why, in conformity with the theory of relativity, the field of gravitation is at the same time a term for the metrical structure of space-time.

When Riemann's condition is "satisfied," then the equations for gravitation must also be "satisfied." In other words, the equations for the field of gravitation are a specialization of Riemann's condition.

You may keep the German manuscript of the Memoir as long as you need it. Naturally, I agree with your proposals concerning revision.

It seems to me that you are not only my only faithful translator, but also my only truly observant reader.

With my cordial greetings
Your

A. Einstein

P.S. I am glad that the French people have not neglected to show their thick-headed leaders where God sits.

den 14. Oktober 1953

Lieber Solo:

Bravo! Ich danke für Ihr tapferes Eintreten für meinen Geldbeutel. Nun können Sie mit Caesar sagen: Veni, Vidi, Vici!

Zu Ihrer ersten Frage: "Disparé" scheint mir eine zutreffende Uebersetzung des Ausdrucks "verlorengeht" zu sein. Die anderen Ausdrücke: " sich nicht eignet", nicht angebracht", sind sinnwidrig. "Nicht möglich ist" wäre nicht deutlich genug, es müsste wenigstens gesagt werden "nicht mehr möglich ist". "Verloren geht" scheint mir aber besser zu sein.

Ihre Bemerkungen zu dem Begriff "Physikalischer Inhalt", den Sie zutreffend mit "contenu physique" übersetzt haben, erscheint mir zutreffend. Die Frage ist nur, ob eine genauere Darlegung das Verständnis nicht eher erschwert als erleichtert. Einerseits nämlich ist die euklidische Geometrie offenbar der Ausdruck primitiver Erfahrungen mit Stäben, Schnüren und Lichtstrahlen. Andererseits entsprechen diese Objekte nur ungenau den geometrischen Begriffen. Von der letzteren Tatsache habe ich eben an der von Ihnen erwähnten Stelle der Vereinfachung halber abgesehen. Ob diese Ungenauigkeiten durch die von ihr erzielten didaktischen Vorteile an der angegebenen Stelle gerechtfertigt sind, darüber kann man verschieden denken. Mir scheint es so.

Auf Ihre Anfrage hin darf ich Ihnen sagen, dass es mir mit Rücksicht auf das vorgerückte Alter recht gut geht, ebenso Margot, wenn man ihre angeborene Schlemiligkeit in Rechnung zieht. Frl. Dukas geht es überhaupt gut ohne Einschränkung.

Indem ich hoffe, dass es sich bei Ihnen Beiden ebenso verhält bin ich mit herzlichen Grüssen

Ihr

A. E

October 14, 1953

Dear Solovine,

Bravo! I thank you for your valiant intercession in favor of my pocketbook. Now you can say with Caesar: *Veni, vidi, vici!*

In answer to your first question: "Disappears" seems to me to be an exact translation of the expression *verloren geht.* The other expressions, *sich nicht eignet* and *nicht angebracht*, are contradictory. *Nicht möglich ist* would not be clear enough; it would have to be *nicht mehr möglich ist.* But *verloren geht* seems better to me.

Your remarks about the notion of *physikalischer Inhalt*, which you correctly translate as "physical content" seem conclusive to me. The only question that arises is whether a more detailed exposition would not make comprehension more difficult rather than easier. On the one hand, Euclidian geometry is manifestly the expression of primitive experiences with sticks, strings, and rays of light. On the other hand, these objects fail to correspond exactly to geometric concepts. For reasons of simplicity, I left out the last consideration in the place mentioned by you. Now, can this lack of precision be justified by the the didactic advantages gained in that passage? Opinions can be different on this point. I think it can.

In reply to you inquiry, I can state that, considering my advanced age, I am fine, as is Margot, considering her congenital bad luck. Miss Dukas is enjoying the best of health, with no reservations.

Hoping that the same holds true for both of you, I am with cordial greetings,

Your,

A. E.

Lieber Solo

Es tut mir schrecklich leid, dass eine so hässliche Reparatur an Ihnen gemacht werden muss. Da Toro hat sich bei Ihnen gemeldet, wie er neulich erzählte. Aber seine Anzeige ist offenbar verloren gegangen. Vielleicht hat der alte Ingrogel die Adresse verwechselt.

Die Korrekturen kann ich schwer beurteilen, da ich den Zusammenhang nicht kenne. Es könnte etwa heissen

„dass die Elektrostatik die elektrischen Wirkungen nur in dem Falle richtig darstellt, dass die elektrischen Massen gegenüber dem Inertialsystem in Ruhe sind."

Bei der ersten der von Ihnen genannten Stellen ist mir eine Entscheidung noch schwieriger. Wenn es sich um die Geometrie handelt, ist „Inhalt" oder „Gehalt" richtiger als „Ursprung". Denn es handelt sich nicht um die Geschichte sondern um das von der Zeit nicht abhängige Wesen der Sache.

Meine herzlichen Wünsche für die schmerzliche „Reparatur". Lassen Sie uns bald wissen, dass es gut gegangen ist. Beste Grüsse an Sie beide

Ihr

A. E.

November 25, 1953

Dear Solo,

I am extremely sorry that you have had to go to so much trouble. Lowe sent a note to you, as he told me recently, but the notice obviously went astray. Perhaps the old carrier pigeon confused your address with another.

It is hard for me to pass on the corrections since I do not know the context. This might be it:

> "...that electrostatics correctly accounts for electrical effects only when the electrical masses are at rest with respect to a system of inertia."

As for the first passage mentioned by you, it is even more difficult for me to decide. In speaking of geometry, "content" or "capacity" are more correct than "origin," for the reference is not to the history but to the nature of the thing, which is independent of time.

My sincere apologies for the regrettable mistake. Let us know soon that everything is again in order.

My very best to both of you.

Your

A. E.

27.II.33.

Lieber Solovine!

Die masslos übertriebene Wertschätzung, die man meiner Lebensarbeit gegenwärtig vielfach zuschreibt, hat auch ihre erfreulichen Seiten. So ist z. B. dem hiesigen Komitee zur Hilfeleistung für Refugié-Gelehrte eine Geldsumme überwiesen worden, deren Verwendung nicht denselben Beschränkungen unterliegt, wie die übrigen Zuwendungen, sondern nach meinem persönlichen Dafürhalten verwendet werden darf. Nun weiss ich, dass Sie durch ein in neueren Jahren sehr verbreitetes Augenübel geplagt sind, das Ihre Thätigkeit sehr erschwert, und das durch eine sehr oft gethätigte Operation behoben werden kann. Ich kann mir keine würdigere Verwendung solcher Mittel denken, als solchen in rastloser geistiger Arbeit ergrauten Menschen, wie Sie es sind, die volle Arbeitskraft zu erhalten.

Schreiben Sie mir deshalb umgehend, wie die Zahlungen aus Boston erfolgen können, ob auf einmal, oder in periodischen Abständen, und vor allem, wie gross der Betrag ist, durch den Ihnen wirklich gedient ist. Die Auszahlung erfolgt dann durch die Schwesteranstalt des hiesigen Komitee's in Paris, sodass Sie keinerlei Scherereien damit haben.

February 27, 1955

Dear Solovine,

The exorbitant price now attached to my life's work on many occasions also has its more pleasant aspects. A certain sum of money, for instance, has been placed at the disposal of a committee set up here to help refugee scholars; this money is not subject to the same restrictions as other emergency funds but is spent at my discretion. I know that you are tormented by an eye ailment, very common at our age, which makes it difficult for you to work and which can be eliminated by an operation that is frequently performed. I can think of no more worthy use of the funds than to offer them to a man who like you, has grown pallid under the stress of constant intellectual labor, in order to preserve his capacity for work.

Write me about this by return mail. Tell me how the payments can best be made, in a lump sum or periodically, and above all, what sum, without any reservations, *can really be of help to you*. The payment will then be made in Paris by the sister institution of the local committee, and in this way there will be no confusion.

Ich habe gerade eine ziemlich schwere Anämie überstanden, über die mich die ärztliche Kunst weggebracht hat. Aber der Karren läuft wieder einigermassen, nur das Gehirn ist etwas sehr eingerostet – der Teufel zählt die Jahre überhaupt gewissenhaft, das muss man anerkennen.

Immerhin hab ich noch eine erhebliche Verbesserung der Verallgemeinerung der Theorie des Gravitationsfeldes gefunden (nicht symmetrische Feldtheorie). Aber auch die so vereinfachten Gleichungen lassen sich wegen der mathematischen Schwierigkeiten noch nicht ~~mit den~~ an Thatsachen prüfen.

Herzlichste Grüsse an Sie und Ihre Frau

Ihr
A. Einstein.

I have just recovered from a rather serious anemic condition, thanks to medical science. The old cart is again in running condition, but the head is a little rusty—the devil counts out the years conscientiously, we must admit.

I have finally managed to introduce another noteworthy improvement into the theory of the gravitational field (theory of the nonsymmetrical field). But not even these simplified equations can be verified by the facts as yet because of mathematical difficulties.

Warmest greetings to you and your wife.

Your

A. Einstein